VEGAN COOKBOOK

Handwritten note:

Tomato Gnocchi
- Gnocchi
- Squash roasted
- Brussel sprouts roasted
- 1 Bottle Oat for Cooking
- Paprika
- Garlic Powder
- Basil
- Onion Powder
- Salt
- Pepper
- Tomato Paste

VEGAN Cookbook

Top 100 Healthy and Delicious Plant-Based Vegan Recipes

Kerry Quinta

CONTENTS

HOW I WENT VEGAN

I never thought I would become a vegan.

That may be strange to hear, considering this is a vegan cookbook, but I want to be honest about my journey. I always rolled my eyes a little at stories about celebrities becoming vegan and all the hoops people jumped through to stick to the diet. I was happy with my meat-and-cheese heavy lifestyle and didn't plan on changing. Then one of my best friends became a vegan.

I was really surprised when she broke the news. She wasn't one to jump on the latest diet trend or make decisions on impulse, so I really wanted to know why she decided to change her life. We had a lot of conversations about the food industry, how animals were treated, the health effects of different diets, and more. She opened my eyes about how food is brought to the table and how plant-based diets can be so much healthier. I didn't immediately decide to join her, but whenever we went out, I was open to vegan restaurants and trying new dishes. When we cooked together, it was always vegan food, and I could see how tasty everything was. I started paying more attention to my own body, too, and noticed how it responded differently to veggie-packed meals without meat. I felt better, and I wanted to always feel that way.

When I decided to become a vegan, I knew it would be a challenge at first, but I don't think I anticipated just how much of a challenge it would be. Everyone's experience is different and many people transition really well, but I was going from a very meat-and-dairy rich diet to a totally plant-based one. It wasn't easy. I started relying on lots of processed and packaged vegan options, and while I was technically following the rules, I knew I wasn't getting all the health benefits of the diet. I wasn't losing the weight I expected and knew I was eating too much sugar. I didn't feel that healthy, energetic glow other vegans talked about. How could I make veganism work for me and depend on real, whole foods?

For me, they key was developing recipes that were based on eating well but still tasted amazing. Being a vegan doesn't have to be a sacrifice and over time I figured out a sustainable way to make veganism work for me. I know it can work for you too.

This book breaks down everything I learned about veganism to help you thrive on a plant-based diet. It isn't the easiest decision to make, but it doesn't have to be hard, either. Healthy, vegan cooking should be fun, and you should never feel like it's taking up all your time. I sincerely hope this cookbook can help you to enjoy everything a vegan lifestyle has to offer.

Yours in good health,

Kerry Quinta

AN INTRODUCTION TO VEGANISM

Every year, more and more people switch to veganism. What does that mean, exactly? For many, it's the natural end to vegetarianism, while others decide to take a leap from a meat-heavy diet to one devoted to plants. When you become a vegan, you eliminate *all* meat and fish from your diet, along with any animal-based products like honey and gelatin. Often, people also stop wearing certain clothes or using certain cosmetics and shampoo. Since this book is about food, however, we'll focus solely on the diet aspect of veganism. This section breaks down how veganism was created, the benefits and risks, and what every vegan should know about food and nutrients.

A BRIEF HISTORY OF VEGANISM

Very early humans might have been vegan, though they didn't have a choice. Before tools and fire, our ancestors ate wild fruits, seeds, nuts, and vegetables. Once they figured out how to hunt, use weapons, and cook with fire, their diet expanded. They killed animals, learning how to preserve their meat, fur, and skin. Eventually, many animals were domesticated for their meat and other products like eggs and milk. As civilization formed, so did ideas about diets and animals. Many began wondering if using animals was morally right or the healthiest option for humans. Ancient Indian and eastern Mediterranean cultures embraced vegetarianism the most, though they were not what we consider "vegans."

Not eating *any* animal products didn't become a thing until the early 1800's, at least in the Western world. One of the earliest mentions of eliminating eggs and dairy along with meat can be found among Percy Bysshe Shelley's circle of friends. The romantic poet stuck to a strict diet, believing plants could cure virtually every disease. Fast forward to 1944 and we finally see the modern understanding of veganism emerge. Donald Watson, a British vegetarian who gave up dairy at 32 years-old, met with others who had chosen this path. They decided that the term "non-dairy vegetarian" wasn't ideal, so they brainstormed a different title. They chose "vegan" and became The Vegan Society, defining themselves as people seeking an end to the "use of animals by man for food, commodities, work, hunting, vivisection, and by all others uses involving exploitation of animal life by man."

Thanks to the work of The Vegan Society, Donald Watson, and vegans worldwide, interest in the diet has exploded over the years. In the US, 1% of consumers said they were vegan in 2014, and in 2017, that percentage rose to 6%. It's no longer unusual to see brands offering vegan alternatives and using the term as a marketing tool. Veganism has gone mainstream.

WHY ARE SO MANY PEOPLE BECOMING VEGANS?

Veganism is clearly becoming more popular, but why? Vegans sing the praises of the diet, sayi 202ng they feel healthier, stronger, and more attractive than ever. They aren't making this stuff up either. There are lots of benefits to a plant-based diet, many of which are consistently supported by science. Here are the top five reasons to become vegan:

Improves your heart health

Animal fats have been linked to heart diseases. When you give up meat, the absence of those fats and presence of more heart-healthy foods helps protect you against hypertension and other heart conditions. Being overweight and overeating are also connected to heart disease, and while vegans are not immune to these problems, studies have shown that the diet can help with weight loss. Why? The healthiest vegan staples, especially vegetables, are rich in satisfying nutrients like fiber, but low in calories.

Improves your digestive health

The importance of good gut health can't be overstated. 80% of your immune system is found in your gut, and if you have frequent tummy troubles, you know how miserable life can be. Large amounts of dairy and meat are linked to a variety of stomach issues as common as constipation and as severe as bowel cancer. By eliminating those foods and increasing your consumption of nutrient-rich vegetables, you can heal your gut. Fermented foods like sauerkraut, tempeh, and sour pickles are especially good for improving and maintaining good gut health.

Improves your bone health

When thinking about health, don't forget your skeleton! While many are concerned about bone health and veganism because you aren't getting calcium through dairy, you actually can easily substitute with vegetables. Dark leafy greens like kale and spinach are packed with calcium, while soy, fruit, and other veggies contain other essential nutrients for bones like potassium and magnesium. Being vegan has another advantage: the diet allows for better calcium absorption.

Lowers the risk of cancer

Diets heavy in meat have been linked to cancer, especially prostate and colon cancer. When you cut those foods out, you are less likely to develop those diseases. A vegan diet is also full of protective nutrients, like fiber and vitamin C. While any type of cancer can occur with any diet, going vegan lowers your risk. If you commit to a vegan diet based on real food and not processed vegan offerings, you are also less likely to develop cancers associated with artificial ingredients, sweeteners, and other additives.

Improves your skin and hair health

Curious about the outward benefits of veganism? Unsaturated fats found in olive oil and avocado keep your cells happy and hydrated, which results in shinier, stronger hair, and glowing skin. Eliminating dairy can also help with acne breakouts and redness. If you take care to eliminate processed and refined vegan foods, you'll enjoy even better results.

DOES VEGANISM COME WITH ANY RISKS?

No diet is perfect. Because veganism is so restrictive, many nutritionists are concerned about its popularity. Are vegan eaters missing out on important nutrients and actually risking their health? Sometimes. It depends on how careful you are. Before deciding if veganism is right for you, it's important to understand the risks. Here are four:

Too little protein

The highest amounts of protein are found in animal sources, so vegans often worry about getting enough. It can be challenging and protein deficiency results in symptoms like fatigue, joint pain, and more. As a vegan, you have to be more intentional about getting good protein. For many, this means taking a supplement like a high-quality powder, though you can get lots of protein from sources like seitan, lentils, and quinoa.

Too little saturated fat

While people often wince when they hear the words "saturated fat," your body needs them. You need cholesterol to produce and balance hormones. Saturated fat also actually helps the liver get rid of fat, which helps with losing weight around your midsection. Saturated fat is also the main type of fat in the brain, so eating foods rich in fat helps the brain's ability to function. Unfortunately for vegans, the best source for saturated fat is meat. To get enough on a plant-based diet, incorporate coconut products (like coconut oil) and olive oil into your meals.

Risk of micronutrient deficiency

One of the main complaints with the vegan diet is that it eliminates so many foods high in essential nutrients. You need to be aware of what they are and find good substitutes. Some nutrients, however, are only found naturally in animal sources. B12 is one of these nutrients, and 90% of vegans are too low. It's important to take supplements and get regular tests to find out if you are deficient.

Can cause digestive problems

While veganism can help with digestive problems, it can also cause them. If you eat too much fiber, it can cause issues like bloating, diarrhea, and cramping. Long-term, too much fiber interferes with the absorption of calcium, iron, and zinc. If you start to experiencing the tell-tale signs of too much fiber, cut back. If you are switching from a diet low in fiber, a short transition period is normal, but if you continue experiencing bloating and cramping, you're probably getting too much.

WHAT VEGANS EAT

What are you allowed to eat on the vegan diet? It's a lot of vegetables, fruit, grains, nuts, seeds, animal substitutes, and more. Here is a list of what every vegan kitchen should include, give or take a few of your favorite ingredients:

Vegetables + fruit

- Dark leafy greens
- Other fresh, in-season vegetables
- Fresh seasonal fruit
- Frozen berries
- Frozen bagged veggies
- Canned tomatoes
- Canned veggies

Grains

- Steel-cut oats
- White rice
- Brown rice
- Whole-wheat pasta
- Vegan-friendly whole-grain bread
- Quinoa

Nuts + seeds

- Dry-roasted almonds
- Dry-roasted pecans
- Macadamia nuts
- Pumpkin seeds
- Sunflower seeds
- Chia seeds
- Nut butter

Dairy-free substitutes

- Nut milk (coconut, almond, cashew, whatever you like)
- Vegan cheese
- Vegan butter
- Coconut milk or soy yogurt

Meat substitutes

- Tofu
- Seitan
- Tempeh
- Mushrooms
- Lentils
- Textured vegetable protein

Beans

- Canned beans
- Dried beans
- Lentils

Cooking/baking supplies

- Vegetable broth
- Full-fat coconut milk
- Organic tomato sauce
- Nutritional yeast
- Spices
- Whole-wheat flour
- Nut flour (almond, coconut)
- White sugar
- Brown sugar
- Arrowroot powder (or cornstarch or tapioca starch)
- Unsweetened applesauce
- Baking powder and baking soda

Condiments/vinegars/oils

- Miso paste
- Tahini
- Bragg soy sauce
- Vegan mayonnaise
- Apple cider vinegar
- Balsamic vinegar
- EVOO
- Extra virgin coconut oil

UNDERSTANDING FOOD SUBSTITUTES

In the list above, you saw what food to buy when you're looking to replace dairy and meat, but let's explore those ingredients in a bit more depth. If you aren't familiar with them, using them to their full potential can be confusing. When you know what to do, however, they can be just as tasty and satisfying as the real deal.

Substituting meat

The easiest (and arguably most popular) meat substitute is tofu. Made from soy, it has a high protein and calcium count. For the best meat texture, go with extra-firm tofu. It is bland, so don't be stingy with spices and seasonings. Tofu can be grilled, broiled, or pan-fried. Before cooking, tofu needs to be pressed so the water it's packed in drains out. Tempeh is another soy option, though it's made from fermented soybeans. It has a firmer, grainer texture than tofu, but is also high in protein. It doesn't need to be pressed. If you want to replace ground meat in a recipe, go with textured vegetable protein, which is made from dehydrated soy.

For those avoiding soy, seitan is made from processed wheat gluten. It's versatile and can be prepared in a variety of ways, such as fried or grilled. It has a very realistic meat texture and easily absorbs flavors. It's also very affordable and packs in a lot of protein.

Substituting eggs

Eggs are tricky because of their unique texture and role in baking. They are an essential binder. There are variety of ingredient combinations that replace eggs, such as water with arrowroot powder or cornstarch. Two tablespoons of cornstarch (or arrowroot) mixed with three tablespoons of water equals one full egg. Chia seeds or ground flax seeds, which get a jelly texture when soaked in water, are also a common egg sub for baking. One tablespoon of chia seeds soaked in three tablespoons of water (for 15 minutes) gets you the equivalent of two eggs. For flax seeds, you need two tablespoons with six tablespoons of water.

To replicate egg whites for meringues and other whipped recipes, aquafaba has become very popular. Aquafaba is the liquid from a can of chickpeas - three tablespoons of the stuff equals one egg white. You'll also see mashed bananas and applesauce used in muffin and pancake recipes, though they don't pack in quite as many nutrients as the seed subs.

Substituting cheese

There are lots of faux cheeses on the market, but many vegans are concerned about how processed they are. If you're looking for other substitutes, consider tofu, cashews, and nutritional yeast. When sliced, tofu is a decent sub for mozzarella or provolone. Smoking it helps add to the illusion, while seasonings like salt are essential. For ricotta or cottage cheese, simply mash up tofu. If you want to try your hand at creating your own cheese sub, try running cashews through a food processor with vinegar or white wine, and seasoning generously with garlic, salt, and lemon juice. You end up with something close to a tasty soft cheese.

For parmesan or just added umami flavor, nutritional yeast is the way to go. It's fortified with B12 and contains lots of protein, as well as minerals like zinc and magnesium. Just sprinkle on anything and everything from pasta to popcorn.

Substituting milk

There are seemingly endless substitutes for milk. Nut milks are actually taking over the industry to the dismay of dairy farmers. Soy milk is the closest in terms of nutrition to dairy milk. It boasts 8-11 grams of protein per cup. Almond milk is also a popular choice, and usually has less sugar and calories than its soy counterpart. The third milk, coconut milk, has important saturated fats for vegans. You'll often see blends of nut milks from brands like Califa farms.

These are just the three most well-known nut milks, but there are others like hemp milk (a complete protein), rice milk, cashew milk, macadamia nut milk, oat milk, and pea milk. Not all plant milks are created equal, so watch for additives like too much sugar.

Substituting butter

For spreading on toast or other baked goods, vegan butter substitutes are the closest to real butter. A lot of people also enjoy avocado (with a little salt) or nut butters. For baking, you can replace butter with olive oil. ¾ cup of olive oil replaces 1 cup of butter. That same ratio applies to pumpkin puree, while applesauce has a 1-1 ratio.

GOOD VEGAN BRANDS

- Amy's frozen entrees
- Annie's vegan snacks and mac 'n cheese
- Aldi's vegan burgers
- Nasoya Organic non-GMO tofu
- Field Roast sausages and cheese
- Upton's Naturals jackfruit
- Tofurkey deli "meat"
- Silk nut milk and yogurt
- Bolthouse Farms pea protein milk
- Califa farms nut milk
- Daiya cheese
- Halo Top vegan high-protein ice creams
- Ben & Jerry's vegan ice creams
- Earth Balance butter spread
- Celsius energy drinks
- Vega protein bars
- Ener-G egg replacer
- Bob's Red Mill's potato starch and tapioca flour, psyllium husk fiber, and baking soda egg replacer
- Bee-Free Honee
- Nutiva organic coconut oil and hemp protein powder
- Garden of Life nutritional supplements

IMPORTANT NUTRIENTS FOR VEGANS

Because you eliminate so many foods on the vegan diet, there are certain minerals and vitamins that you risk missing out on. Most can be found in real foods, though a high-quality supplement might be necessary. Here are the nutrients to watch for:

Iron

If you don't get enough iron, you'll most likely experience weakness, fatigue, and dizziness. Low iron can also lead to anemia if it isn't addressed. To get more iron in your diet, be sure to stock up on dried beans and dark leafy greens. You can also get a cast-iron skillet, which will add small amounts of iron into food you cook.

Vitamin B12

A B12 deficiency causes fatigue, shortness of breath, and gut problems. On the serious side, it can lead to nerve damage and loss of vision. You can get B12 from nutritional yeast, fortified soy, and seaweed.

Calcium

Without enough calcium, you might experience a poor appetite, fatigue, muscle cramps, and weak fingernails and toenails. Long-term, your brain and bones suffer. To get enough, be sure to eat dark leafy greens, tahini, and tofu.

Zinc

When you're low in zinc, you'll suffer from a poor appetite, fatigue, and gut problems. Long-term, your immune system gets hit the hardest, so you'll have trouble recovering from illnesses and injuries. Zinc can be found in soy, spinach, legumes, and whole grains.

Vitamin D

Without vitamin D, you'll experience fatigue, back pain, and muscle pain. Eventually, things get worse, and your bone health is affected, as well as your heart and brain. Naturally, vitamin D is only found in animal products, but lots of vegan-friendly foods are fortified with it. Look for fortified almond milk, fortified soy milk, and fortified orange juice. You can also get a bit by spending time outdoors in the sun for just 10-15 minutes a day. It should be on your bare skin, so don't wear sunscreen. Be sure to never get sunburned, though.

Omega-3 fatty acids

A lack of omega-3s can increase your risk for diseases like heart disease, dementia, and more. Most people get enough from your their diet, but when you're vegan, you eliminate a lot of those foods. There are three main fatty acids the body needs: ALA, DHA, and EPA. ALA and DHA can be found in soy, ground flaxseed, and walnuts. EPA only appears in animal products, so you'll have to take a supplement.

LENTILS AND BEANS

Contents

Vegetable Potato Fritters with Red Lentils

Serves: 12 / Preparation time: 10 minutes / Cooking time: 15 minutes

For the vegetable potato fritters:

3/4 cup red lentils

1 small red onion, chopped

2 cloves of garlic

2 medium-sized potatoes (raw)

1 medium-sized carrot

5 tablespoons all-purpose flour

1/2 teaspoon smoked paprika powder

1 teaspoon regular paprika powder

1 teaspoon majoram

salt

black pepper, to taste

For the sriracha mayonnaise:

3 tablespoons vegan mayonnaise

1 teaspoon tomato paste

1 teaspoon garlic powder

1/2 teaspoon smoked paprika powder

salt

black pepper, to taste

sriracha sauce, to taste

- Cook the red lentils according to the instructions on the package. Peel and grate the potatoes and the carrot.
- In a large bowl, combine them with the cooked red lentils, the garlic, the onion, the flour, and the spices and stir well.
- Heat some oil in a large pan, and add about 1 1/2 heaped tablespoons for each fritter. Cook them on medium heat in a son-sticky pan for three to four minutes on each side. Alternatively, you can also make them in the oven for an oil-free version (about 20 minutes, flipping halfway).
- For the vegan sriracha mayonnaise, combine all ingredients and stir well.
- Serve the fritters with a green salad and the sriracha mayonnaise. Enjoy!

Per Serving: Calories: 101; Total Fat: 1g; Saturated Fat: 0.1g; Protein: 5g; Carbs: 18g; Fiber: 3g; Sugar: 2g

Vegan Lentil Chili

Serves: 6 / Preparation time: 10 minutes / Cooking time: 45 minutes

2 cups yellow onion diced

1 TBSP olive oil

1 large green bell pepper diced

1 large red bell pepper diced

2 jalapeños plus extra to garnish

2-4 cloves garlic minced

1 cup corn frozen or fresh

15 oz can spicy chili beans with sauce

1 cup black beans (drained and rinsed)

2 TBSP chili powder

1 TBSP cumin

1 tsp dried oregano

1/2 tsp smoked paprika plus extra to taste

salt and pepper to taste

2 cups veggie broth

1 cup dried red lentils

2 cups crushed tomatoes

EXTRAS:

diced jalapenos or cayenne pepper for a kick

veggie broth or tomato sauce to adjust thickness if desired

all the tasty toppings your heart desires!

TOPPING INSPIRATION:

sliced or diced jalapeños

chopped red onion

fresh pico de gallo or salsa

sliced avocado

fresh cilantro

sour cream or greek yogurt if vegetarian/t-rex

shredded cheddar cheese if vegetarian/t-rex

crushed tortilla chips

corn chips

corn bread crumbles

- Bring a large pot to medium heat and add a drizzle of your favorite cooking oil. Sauté your onion until edges are golden, then add your garlic, bell pepper, and jalapeño. Cook until peppers are tender, approx. 5 minutes.
- Next add veggie broth, crushed tomatoes, corn, chili beans, black beans, and spices; stir to mix. Let mixture come to a boil and add your dried red lentils. Once boiling, reduce heat to medium-low and simmer, covered, for 25-30 minutes.
- The longer you let it cook the more pronounced the flavor will be. Feel free to cook a little longer if time permits, up to you! Scoop out a bowlful, pile on the toppings, sit back, and enjoy!

Per Serving: Calories: 321; Total Fat: 4g; Saturated Fat: 1g; Protein: 16g; Carbs: 56g; Fiber: 18g; Sugar: 1g

Tacos with Lentil Walnut Meat

Serves: 6 / Preparation time: 30 minutes / Cooking time: 20 minutes

For the lentil walnut meat:

1 cup walnuts

1 cup brown lentils

1 tablespoon olive oil

1/2 onion, finely chopped

1 tablespoon tomato paste

1/2 cup diced tomatoes

1 teaspoon cumin

1 teaspoon paprika powder

2 teaspoons oregano

salt

black pepper

For the vegan sour cream:

1 cup cashews, soaked for 30 minutes

1/4 cup lemon juice

1 clove of garlic

salt

black pepper

For the tacos:

1 tomato

1 avocado

1 cup kidney beans

1 cup corn

lettuce

about 8 taco shells

- Cook the lentils according to the instructions. Drain and set aside. In a medium pan, roast the walnuts without oil for about 2 minutes or until they're lightly golden. Put the walnuts and the cooked lentils in a food processor and process until chopped. Make sure to leave some texture!
- In a medium pan, heat the olive oil over medium heat and sautée the onions for about 3 minutes. Then add the lentil walnut mixture and stir in the tomato paste. Cook for 2 minutes. Add the diced tomatoes and the spices (paprika powder, cumin, oregano, salt, and pepper).
- Make the sour cream: Drain the cashews and put all ingredients in a food processor and process until smooth. Season with salt and pepper.
- Fill the taco shells with the lentil walnut meat, tomato, avocado, kidney beans, corn, and lettuce and top with sour cream.

Per Serving: Calories: 321; Total Fat: 4g; Saturated Fat: 1g; Protein: 16g; Carbs: 56g; Fiber: 18g; Sugar: 1g

Lentil Loaf

Serves: 6 / Preparation time: 15 minutes / Cooking time: 45 minutes

2 cups cooked French lentils	2 tablespoons flax meal
1/2 yellow onion, diced	1 tablespoon dried parsley
2 carrots, diced	¼ teaspoon salt
2 celery stalks, diced	¼ teaspoon pepper
1/2 cup diced red bell pepper	½ cup quick oats
1 ¼ cup diced crimini mushrooms	½ cup breadcrumbs
2 cloves garlic, minced	3 bell peppers, halved and seeded (optional)
2 tablespoons tomato paste	1/3 cup ketchup
1 tablespoon bbq sauce	pinch brown or coconut sugar

- Preheat the oven to 350 degrees F. Line a baking sheet with parchment paper. In a large skillet over medium heat, saute onion, carrots, celery, pepper, and mushrooms with a pinch of salt and pepper until softened. Add the garlic and saute another minute longer.
- In a food processor, pulse together the lentils, cooked vegetables, tomato paste, bbq sauce, flax meal, parsley, salt, pepper, oats, and breadcrumbs. You may have to work in batches if your food processor is small. Do not puree, but blend into a chunky dough. You want some bits of veggies for texture.
- Form the dough into a ball and place on the prepared cookie sheet. Form into a "loaf" shape as shown in the pictures. Alternatively, fill bell pepper halves with the lentil mixture and place in a baking dish. Bake for 35 minutes. Remove from the oven and spread the ketchup on top. Sprinkle with sugar to help caramelize the topping. Bake for another 10 minutes. Let the lentil loaf cool at least 10 minutes as it firms up during this time.

Per Serving: Calories: 190; Total Fat: 2g; Saturated Fat: 0g; Protein: 10g; Carbs: 35g; Fiber: 8g; Sugar: 1g

Turkish Lentil Bulgur Wheat Patties

Serves: 4 / Preparation time: 15 minutes / Cooking time: 30 minutes

175 g Red Lentils	Salad
225 g Bulgur Wheat	1/4 Cucumber chopped
1 Onion finely chopped	1 Red Pepper chopped
1 tbsp Chilli Paste	3 medium Tomatoes chopped
1 tbsp Olive Oil	1/2 Red Onion chopped
2 tsp Cumin	Small bunch Fresh Parsley chopped
100 g Rocket (Arugula)	Small bunch Fresh Mint chopped
Salt and Pepper	2 tbsp Olive Oil
Olive Oil for frying	

- Put the lentils in a saucepan with 250ml water and bring to a boil then simmer for 10 minutes. Remove from the heat and add the bulgur wheat, chilli paste, cumin, olive oil, a big pinch of salt and 120ml (1/2 cup) of boiling water. Mix together then let sit for 15 minutes until all the water has been absorbed.
- Heat a drizzle of olive oil over a medium heat and fry the onion for 5 minutes until soft. Allow to cool for a few minutes then add to the lentil mixture and stir together.
- In the pan you used for the onions heat another drizzle of oil. Make small patties out of the mixture. Fry for 3-5 minutes on each side adding more oil as necessary.
- For the salad, mix together all of the ingredients. Serve the patties with the rocket, salad and pittas. They're great with hummus and chilli sauce too!

Per Serving: Calories: 475; Total Fat: 12g; Saturated Fat: 1g; Protein: 19g; Carbs: 75g; Fiber: 65g; Sugar: 5g

Lentil Burger with Basil Mayonnaise

Serves: 4 / Preparation time: 15 minutes / Cooking time: 60 minutes

For the vegan lentil patties:

1 cup brown lentils

7 oz firm tofu (one block)

2 tablespoons tomato paste

8 sun-dried tomatoes

1 tablespoon olive oil

1 small onion, chopped

1/2 cup whole wheat flour

3/4 cup rolled oats

1 carrot, grated

1 teaspoon oregano

1 teaspoon thyme

1 teaspoon basil

1 teaspoon soy sauce

1 teaspoon mustard

salt

black pepper

For the basil mayonnaise:

6-8 tablespoons store-bought or homemade vegan mayonnaise

about 10 basil leaves

For the rosemary fries:

about 8 large potatoes, cut into even wedges

1 teaspoon rosemary

2 tablespoon olive oil

sea salt

For the burger:

buns

arugula

tomatoes

- Cook the brown lentils according to the instructions on the package.
- Make the rosemary fries: Preheat the oven to 475 degrees Fahrenheit. Line a baking sheet with parchment paper and put the potatoe wedges on top. Drizzle with olive oil and sprinkle with rosemary and salt. Bake for about 40 minutes or until crispy and brown.
- Make the basil mayonnaise: In a food processor, combine the vegan mayonnaise and the basil leaves and process until smooth.
- Put about 1/4 of the cooked lentils in a food processor together with the tofu, the mustard, the sun-dried tomatoes, and the tomato paste. Process until well combined.
- In a small skillet, head the olive oil and sauté the onion for about 3 minutes or until it is translucent.
- Add the remaining cooked lentils, the onion, the rolled oats, the whole wheat flour, the grated carrot, the spices, soy sauce, and mustard to the lentil-tofu mixture and stir well. Season with salt and pepper and form about 4 burger patties.
- In a large pan, heat some olive oil and bake the patties for about 3 minutes on each side or until they are slightly brown.
- Serve on buns with the basil mayonnaise, arugula, and tomatoes.

Per Serving: Calories: 127; Total Fat: 2g; Saturated Fat: 0.1g; Protein: 6g; Carbs: 25g; Fiber: 5g; Sugar: 3g

Lentil Shepherd's Pie

Serves: 4 / Preparation time: 15 minutes / Cooking time: 30 minutes

Mashed potatoes
4 medium potatoes, peeled
1/4 cup almond milk
1 tbsp vegan butter or oil
1/4 tsp salt
Lentils
1 medium onion
1 large carrot
1 celery stalk
2 garlic cloves (skins removed)

1 tbsp avocado oil (or vegetable oil)
pinch of salt & pepper
1/4 cup red wine to deglaze
1 1/2 cups lentils (canned or pre-cooked)
1/2 cup green peas
3 tbsp tomato paste
1/2 cup-3/4 cup vegetable broth
1 tsp thyme
1 tsp garlic powder
salt & pepper to taste

- Chop the onion, carrot and celery large chunks and then add to a food processor along with the garlic cloves. Pulse until chopped into small pieces.
- Heat the avocado oil in a non-stick pan on medium-high heat. Add the vegetable mixture to the pan with a pinch of salt and pepper and let brown, stirring constantly for 6-7 minutes until the veggies are nice and brown. (They will cook down a lot)
- Once the veggies are browned, add the red wine, stirring until the liquid is evaporated, then reduce heat to medium.
- Add the lentils, peas, tomato paste, 1/2 cup vegetable broth, thyme, garlic powder and salt and pepper and stir together letting cook for 5 minutes on medium-low heat. If the lentils become too dry add the remaining 1/4 cup broth if needed
- Remove from heat and set aside.
- Chop the potatoes into large chunks and add to a pot of boiling water.
- Boil for about 10 minutes, or until potatoes are tender.
- Drain the water, then add the almond milk, butter and salt and mash with a potato masher.
- Scoop the lentil mixture into ramekins or baking dish and top with the mashed potatoes
- Bake at 400 degrees F for 15 minutes.
- *Optional* turn the oven on broil for 2 minutes to make the tops crispy

Per Serving: Calories: 547; Total Fat: 8g; Saturated Fat: 4g; Protein: 25g; Carbs: 94g; Fiber: 31g; Sugar: 11g

Creamy Red Lentil Dahl

Serves: 4 / Preparation time: 15 minutes / Cooking time: 30 minutes

1 large onion , chopped finely

4 large garlic cloves , chopped finely

2 tablespoons fresh ginger , finely chopped or grated

1 teaspoon red chili pepper flakes , add up to a teaspoon extra if you like it a spicy. You can use 1 fresh small red chili if you prefer

½ teaspoon ground cinnamon

2 slightly heaping teaspoons turmeric

1 teaspoon fennel seeds

1 teaspoon cumin seeds

1 teaspoon ground coriander

1 teaspoon ground pepper, add more to taste if necessary at the end

2 teaspoons salt , add more to taste if necessary at the end

400g / 2 cups red lentils , dried. No need to soak

3 large tomatoes , chopped into small chunks

1 can / 400 mls / a little under 1¾ cup coconut milk , full fat or light

840mls / 3½ cups water , plus a 3 - 4 tablespoons for sautéing the onion and garlic

- Add 3 tablespoons of water (or 1 tablespoon of oil if you prefer) to a large pan and place over a medium heat. Once the pan is hot add the chopped onion and sauté for about 5 - 10 minutes until translucent. Stir frequently and add a drop or two of water as you need to to stop them sticking.
- Add the chopped garlic & ginger to the pan and cook for about 1 minute longer.
- Add the chili and spices and cook them out for a minute or two then add the lentils. Toast the lentils gently for a few minutes, stirring frequently to stop them sticking.
- Add the chopped tomatoes, water and coconut milk, stir well and bring to a gentle simmer.
- Turn down to medium low, and continue to simmer for around another 25-30 minutes, stirring every 5 minutes or so, until the lentils are breaking down and the sauce is nice and thick.

Per Serving: Calories: 300; Total Fat: 5g; Saturated Fat: 5g; Protein: 17g; Carbs: 50g; Fiber: 10g; Sugar: 5g

Lentil Meatballs

Serves: 4 / Preparation time: 15 minutes / Cooking time: 30 minutes

Lentil Meatballs
1 tablespoon olive oil
1/2 cup onion, finely chopped
2 cloves garlic, minced
1 teaspoon parsley
1/4 teaspoon dried thyme
1/4 teaspoon paprika
1/2 cup dried lentils
2 cups water or vegetable broth
1 cup walnuts, finely chopped
2 tablespoons oatflour
2 tablespoons ground flax seeds
2 tablespoons nutritional yeast flakes
2 teaspoons Bragg's liquid aminos
1/2 teaspoon salt

Creamy Cashew Gravy
1/2 cup cashews, soaked for 1 hour then drained
2 cups water
2 tablespoons nutritional yeast flakes
1 teaspoon onion powder
1 clove garlic, chopped
1 tablespoon arrowroot powder, or cornstarch
3 tablespoons Bragg's liquid aminos
1/2 teaspoon dried thyme
1/2 teaspoon paprika
1/2 teaspoon Italian seasoning
Pinch of Cayenne pepper

- Heat oil in a saucepan over medium-high heat. Add onion and cook until soft, about 3 minutes. Stir in garlic, thyme, parsley, paprika, and lentils to coat.
- Add water and bring to boil over medium heat. Reduce heat to simmer and cover the pot. Cook until lentils are tender and water has completely evaporated about 30 minutes. (Make sure lentils are dry and not soggy)
- Transfer lentil mixture to a large bowl and set aside. Using a food processor, process/pulse walnuts until finely chopped. Stir walnuts into lentils along with the *oat flour, flaxseeds, yeast flakes, Bragg's Liquid Aminos and salt.
- Preheat oven 400 degrees F. Prepare baking sheet with lightly greased parchment paper.
- Scoop mixture, using about 1-2 tablespoons. Form into balls and placing them on prepared sheets in a single layer until mixture is all gone. Bake for 30 minutes or until brown and crispy on the outside.
- To Prepare Cashew Gravy
- Combine cashews, water, yeast flakes, onion powder, garlic, arrowroot, Bragg's Liquid Aminos in a high-speed blender and process until smooth.
- Pour sauce into a saucepan and add thyme, Italian seasonings, paprika. Heat on medium-high, stirring constantly with a wire whisk until sauce thickens.
- Place meat balls in serving plate. Pour gravy on top and garnish with chopped parsley.

Per Serving: Calories: 330; Total Fat: 21g; Saturated Fat: 5g; Protein: 13g; Carbs: 25g; Fiber: 10g; Sugar: 5g

Lentil Chickpea Yellow Curry

Serves: 8 / Preparation time: 5 minutes / Cooking time: 20 minutes

1/2 cup lentils

1 can 14 oz chickpeas

2 14 oz cans coconut milk

6 garlic cloves, peeled and chopped

3 Tbs yellow curry paste

1 onion

salt pepper to taste

OPTIONAL ADD-ONS

lemon juice

chopped bell pepper

2 tbs cashew butter

- Heat a large casserole. Use a bit coconut oil or just vegetable broth for frying the onions and garlic. Do this for at least 3 minutes, before you add coconut milk and lentils, yellow curry paste. Then cook this for 20 minutes – please not longer. We don't want the ingredients mushy or overcooked. Just 5 minutes from the end, add chickpeas.
- Choose your optional add ons and customize your curry to your liking. Serve into bowls and enjoy

Per Serving: Calories: 468; Total Fat: 14g; Saturated Fat: 3g; Protein: 22g; Carbs: 75g; Fiber: 21g; Sugar: 3g

Taco Salad with Lentil Walnut Meat

Serves: 4 / Preparation time: 15 minutes / Cooking time: 30 minutes

For the lentil walnut meat:

1 cup walnuts

1 cup brown lentils

1 tablespoon olive oil

1/2 onion

1 tablespoon tomato paste

1/2 cup diced tomatoes

1 teaspoon cumin

1 teaspoon paprika powder

2 teaspoons oregano

For the cashew sour cream:

1 cup cashews, soaked for 30 minutes

1/4 cup lemon juice

1 clove of garlic

For the salad:

1 cup corn

1 cup black beans

lettuce, roughly chopped

2 green onions, cut into rings

1/2 red onion, cut into half rings

1 cup nachos

1 avocado, cut into slices

1/2 cup fresh cilantro

1 tomato

3/4 cup tomato salsa

- Cook the lentils according to the instructions. Drain and set aside. In a medium pan, roast the walnuts without oil for about 2 minutes or until they're lightly golden. Put the walnuts and the cooked lentils in a food processor and process until chopped. Make sure to leave some texture!
- In a medium pan, heat the olive oil over medium heat and sautée the onions for about 3 minutes. Then add the lentil walnut mixture and stir in the tomato paste. Cook for 2 minutes. Add the diced tomatoes and the spices (paprika powder, cumin, oregano, salt, and pepper).
- Make the sour cream: Drain the cashews and put all ingredients in a food processor and process until smooth. Season with salt and pepper.
- In a large bowl, combine the lettuce, the corn, the tomato, the avocado, the salsa, and the black beans. Serve with the lentil walnut meat, cashew sour cream, and the nachos on top and sprinkle with green onions, red onions, and fresh cilantro.

Per Serving: Calories: 468; Total Fat: 14g; Saturated Fat: 3g; Protein: 22g; Carbs: 75g; Fiber: 21g; Sugar: 3g

Hearty Vegan Mushroom, Ale & Lentil Pie

Serves: 4 / Preparation time: 15 minutes / Cooking time: 25 minutes

Olive oil

10 small shallots, halved

1 tsp garlic purée / ready-chopped garlic

2 tbsp tomato purée

75 g puy lentils, washed and drained

300 g chestnut or flat mushrooms, sliced thickly

20 g dried porcini mushrooms

275 ml brown ale (check it is vegan)

200 ml vegetable stock

50 g baby spinach

Cornflower and dariy-free margarine made to a paste (to thicken)

Ready-made puff pastry (check it is vegan)

Soya milk to glaze

- Heat a little olive oil in a pan, add shallots and cook gently until brown. Reduce heat, add the garlic and cook for two more minutes.
- Stir in tomato purée, lentils, and mushrooms. Turn up heat and cook for five minutes.
- Stir in the brown ale and 100ml of the stock. Cover, bring to the boil and simmer for 30 minutes.
- Meanwhile, soak the porcini mushrooms in 200ml warm water for 20 minutes, drain (reserving the soaking liquor) and chop roughly. Add both the porcini and the soaking liquor to the pan.
- Preheat the oven to 180ºC/350ºF/Gas Mark 4.
- Simmer for a further 10 minutes, using the remaining stock or the cornflour and margarine paste to adjust the consistency until a thick gravy-like pie filling is achieved.
- Stir through the baby spinach, and spoon the mixture into the pie dish. Brush the edges with a little soya milk and cover with rolled puff pastry.
- Brush the pie top with soya milk and bake for 20 minutes or until pastry top is golden and well risen. Serve immediately.

Per Serving: Calories: 385; Total Fat: 5g; Saturated Fat: 4g; Protein: 8g; Carbs: 31g; Fiber: 4g; Sugar: 1g

Lentil Salad with Spinach and Pomegranate

Serves: 4 / Preparation time: 15 minutes / Cooking time: 25 minutes

For the vegan lentil salad:

3 cups cooked brown lentils I usually cook them the night before. Or if you like you can also use canned lentils.

1 avocado, cut into slices

2-3 handfuls fresh spinach

1/2 cup walnuts, roughly chopped

2 small apples, cut into small pieces

1 pomegranate

For the tahini orange dressing:

3 tablespoons tahini

2 tablespoons olive oil

1 clove of garlic

6 tablespoons water

4 tablespoons orange juice

2 teaspoons orange zest

salt

black pepper

- Cook the lentils according to the instructions on the package.
- Cut the pomegranate into halves and remove the seeds. I like to do this in a bowl of water because then it doesn't get all messy. Fill a large bowl with water. Place halved pomegranate into the water. Use your fingers to break the seeds out. Remove the white fiber that floats at the top of the water.
- Put all ingredients into a big salad bowl.
- Make the dressing: Place all ingredients into a food processor or blender and process until smooth.
- Pour the dressing over the lentil salad.

Per Serving: Calories: 385; Total Fat: 5g; Saturated Fat: 4g; Protein: 8g; Carbs: 31g; Fiber: 4g; Sugar: 1g

Carrot Lentil Hot Dogs

Serves: 4 / Preparation time: 15 minutes / Cooking time: 25 minutes

200 g dried red lentils rinsed

700 ml vegetable stock

1 tsp olive oil

1 onion finely diced

2 carrots grated

1 ½ tsp smoked paprika

1 tsp garlic powder

salt and pepper

150 g plain flour

2 tsp olive oil

- Cook the lentils in the stock for 10 minutes or until tender, then drain.
- Meanwhile, heat the oil in a frying pan over a medium heat, then add the onion and sautee for a few minutes until translucent but not browned. Add the grated carrot and sautee for 3-5 minutes until soft.
- Add the cooked lentils, carrot mixture, spices, salt and pepper to a food processor and whiz until it's thick and well combined.
- Tip the mixture into a bowl and mix in 3 tablespoons of the flour. Add more flour, a tablespoon at a time, until a thick and manageable consistency. You may not need all of the flour.
- Roll into hot dog-like shapes, place on a plate, cover and refrigerate for at least 30 minutes.
- Heat 1 tsp of the oil in a frying pan over a medium/low heat and add some of the hot dogs. Fry, gently turning often, until golden. Repeat in batches.
- Serve in a hot dog bun.

Per Serving: Calories: 183; Total Fat: 3g; Saturated Fat: 1g; Protein: 8g; Carbs: 33g; Fiber: 8g; Sugar: 2g

Lemony Lentil and Chickpea Salad with Radish and Herbs

Serves: 4 / Preparation time: 20 minutes / Cooking time: 25 minutes

2 cups dried black beluga lentils or French green lentils

2 large garlic cloves, halved lengthwise

2 tablespoons olive oil

Lemon dressing

¼ cup fresh lemon juice (about 2 medium lemons' worth)

2 tablespoons olive oil

1 teaspoon Dijon mustard

1 teaspoon honey or maple syrup

1 clove garlic, pressed or minced

¼ teaspoon fine-grain sea salt

Freshly ground black pepper, to taste

Salad

1 can (15 ounces) chickpeas, rinsed and drained, or 1 ½ cups cooked chickpeas

1 big bunch of radishes, sliced thin and roughly chopped

¼ cup chopped fresh, leafy herbs, chopped (combination of mint and dill recommended)

Optional garnishes: sliced avocado, crumbled feta or goat cheese, handful of fresh leafy greens

- To cook the lentils: Pick over the lentils to remove any bits of debris. Rinse the lentils under running water in a mesh colander. In a medium pot, combine the lentils, halved garlic cloves, olive oil and 4 cups water. Bring the water to a boil, then reduce heat to a gentle simmer and cook until the lentils are cooked through and tender, which will take somewhere between 20 to 35 minutes. Drain the lentils and discard the garlic cloves.
- To make the dressing: Whisk together the ingredients in a small bowl. If you're using pre-steamed lentils instead of cooking your own, add an extra clove of minced garlic and an extra tablespoon of olive oil.
- In a large serving bowl, combine the lentils, chickpeas, chopped radishes and herbs. Drizzle in the dressing and toss to combine. Serve with avocado, crumbled cheese or fresh greens if you'd like.

Per Serving: Calories: 183; Total Fat: 3g; Saturated Fat: 1g; Protein: 8g; Carbs: 33g; Fiber: 8g; Sugar: 2g

Lebanese Lemon-Parsley Bean Salad

Serves: 4 / Preparation time: 15 minutes / Cooking time: 15 minutes

2 cans (15 ounces each) red kidney beans, rinsed and drained, or 3 cups cooked kidney beans

1 can (15 ounces) chickpeas, rinsed and drained, or 1 ½ cups cooked chickpeas

1 small red onion, diced

2 stalks celery, sliced in half or thirds lengthwise and chopped

1 medium cucumber, peeled, seeded and diced

¾ cup chopped fresh parsley

2 tablespoons chopped fresh dill or mint

¼ cup olive oil

¼ cup lemon juice (about 1 ½ lemons)

3 cloves garlic, pressed or minced

¾ teaspoon salt

Small pinch red pepper flakes

- In a serving bowl, combine the prepared kidney beans, chickpeas, onion, celery, cucumber, parsley and dill (or mint).
- Make the lemon dressing: In a small bowl, whisk together the olive oil, lemon juice, garlic, salt and pepper flakes until emulsified. Pour dressing over the bean and vegetable mixture and toss thoroughly.
- Serve immediately for the most flavor, or let it marinate in the refrigerator, covered, for a couple of hours or longer. Leftovers should keep well, covered and refrigerated, for several days. If necessary, wake up leftovers with a little sprinkle of salt or drizzle of lemon juice.

Per Serving: Calories: 300; Total Fat: 10g; Saturated Fat: 2g; Protein: 11g; Carbs: 40g; Fiber: 15g; Sugar: 1g

Roasted Cauliflower and Lentil Tacos with Creamy Chipotle Sauce

Serves: 4 / Preparation time: 15 minutes / Cooking time: 25 minutes

Cauliflower

1 large head of cauliflower, sliced into bite-sized florets

2 to 3 tablespoons olive oil

Salt and freshly ground black pepper

Seasoned lentils

1 tablespoon olive oil

1 cup chopped yellow or white onion

2 large garlic cloves, pressed or minced

2 tablespoons tomato paste

½ teaspoon ground cumin

½ teaspoon chili powder

¾ cup brown lentils, picked over for debris and rinsed

2 cups vegetable broth or water

Chipotle sauce

⅓ cup mayonnaise

2 tablespoons lime juice

2 to 3 tablespoons adobo sauce (from a can of chipotle peppers) or chipotle hot sauce to taste

Salt and freshly ground black pepper, to taste

Everything else

8 small, round corn tortillas

½ cup packed fresh cilantro leaves (cilantro haters, substitute some fresh spring greens instead)

- To roast the cauliflower: Preheat oven to 425 degrees Fahrenheit. Toss cauliflower florets with enough olive oil to cover them in a light, even layer of oil. Season with salt and pepper and arrange the florets in a single layer on a large, rimmed baking sheet. Roast for 30 to 35 minutes, tossing halfway, until the florets are deeply golden on the edges.
- Warm the olive oil in a medium-sized pot over medium heat. Sauté the onion and garlic with a dash of salt for about 5 minutes, until the onions are softened and turning translucent. Add the tomato paste, cumin and chili powder and sauté for another minute, stirring constantly. Add the lentils and the vegetable broth or water. Raise heat and bring the mixture to a gentle simmer. Cook, uncovered, for 20 minutes to 45 minutes, until the lentils are tender and cooked through. Reduce heat as necessary to maintain a gentle simmer, and add more broth or water if the liquid evaporates before the lentils are done. Once the lentils are done cooking, drain off any excess liquid, then cover and set aside.
- To prepare the chipotle sauce, just whisk together the ingredients and set aside (if you have no choice but to use whole chipotle peppers from the can, use a blender to purée it all).
- Warm tortillas individually in a pan over medium heat. Stack the warm tortillas and cover them with a tea towel if you won't be serving the tacos immediately.
- Once all of your components are ready, you can assemble your tacos! Top each tortilla with the lentil mixture, cauliflower, a drizzle of chipotle sauce and a generous sprinkle of chopped cilantro.

Per Serving: Calories: 559; Total Fat: 27g; Saturated Fat: 6g; Protein: 17g; Carbs: 69g; Fiber: 13g; Sugar: 10g

Roasted Broccoli, Arugula and Lentil Salad

Serves: 4 / Preparation time: 20 minutes / Cooking time: 30 minutes

Salad

1 large bunch of broccoli

¾ pound Brussels sprouts (or more broccoli)

2 tablespoons extra-virgin olive oil

¼ teaspoon fine sea salt

½ cup black beluga lentils (or green/Puy lentils), picked through for debris and rinsed

1 ¼ cups water

4 big handfuls of arugula

½ cup freshly grated Parmesan cheese

Lemon Dressing

2 tablespoons extra-virgin olive oil

1 tablespoon lemon juice, to taste

1 teaspoon honey

1 teaspoon Dijon mustard

1 clove garlic, pressed or minced

Pinch of red pepper flakes

¼ teaspoon fine sea salt

Freshly ground black pepper, to taste

- Preheat oven to 425 degrees Fahrenheit and line your largest rimmed baking sheet with parchment paper for easy-clean-up. Cut the broccoli florets into bite-sized pieces. Trim the ends off the sprouts; cut the small sprouts in two through the stem, and the large sprouts into quarters.
- Toss the florets and sprouts in the olive oil so they are lightly coated, and sprinkle with the salt. Spread the florets and sprouts in a single layer on the baking sheet (be sure not to overcrowd). Bake for 24 to 28 minutes, tossing halfway, until the vegetables are crisp-tender and well caramelized on the edges.
- In the meantime, bring the water to a boil in a medium saucepan. Stir in the lentils. Reduce the heat, cover and simmer for 20 to 25 minutes, until the lentils are tender but still retain their shape. Drain off any excess water.
- Whisk together the vinaigrette ingredients while the roasted vegetables and lentils cool a bit.
- In a large serving bowl, combine the roasted vegetables, cooked lentils and arugula. Drizzle with vinaigrette, sprinkle in the Parmesan and toss well. Taste and add more lemon juice (for more zing), salt (for more overall flavor), and/or pepper, if needed. This salad is best served immediately.

Per Serving: Calories: 559; Total Fat: 27g; Saturated Fat: 6g; Protein: 17g; Carbs: 69g; Fiber: 13g; Sugar: 10g

Kale, Black Bean and Avocado Burrito Bowl

Serves: 4 / Preparation time: 20 minutes / Cooking time: 30 minutes

Brown rice
1 cup brown rice, rinsed (short grain/arborio or long grain/basmati recommended)
¼ teaspoon salt
Lime marinated kale
1 bunch curly kale, ribs removed and chopped into small, bite-sized pieces
¼ cup lime juice
2 tablespoons olive oil
½ jalapeño, seeded and finely chopped
½ teaspoon cumin
¼ teaspoon salt
Avocado salsa verde
1 avocado, pitted and sliced into big chunks
½ cup mild salsa verde (any good green salsa will do)

½ cup fresh cilantro leaves (a few stems are ok)
2 tablespoons lime juice
Seasoned black beans
2 cans black beans, rinsed and drained (or 4 cups cooked black beans)
1 shallot, finely chopped (or ⅓ cup chopped red onion)
3 cloves garlic, pressed or minced
¼ teaspoon chili powder
¼ teaspoon cayenne pepper (optional)
Garnish
Cherry tomatoes, sliced into thin rounds
Hot sauce (optional)

- Cook the rice: Bring a big pot of water to a boil, dump in rinsed brown rice and boil, uncovered, for 30 minutes. Turn off the heat, drain the rice and return it to the pot. Cover and let the rice steam in the pot for 10 minutes, then fluff the rice with a fork and season with ¼ teaspoon salt, or more to taste.
- Make the kale salad: Whisk together the lime juice, olive oil, chopped jalapeño, cumin and salt. Toss the chopped kale with the lime marinade in a mixing bowl.
- Make the avocado salsa verde: In a food processor or blender, combine the avocado chunks, salsa verde, cilantro and lime juice and blend well.
- Warm the beans: In a saucepan, warm 1 tablespoon olive oil over medium-low heat. Sauté the shallot and garlic until fragrant, then add the beans, chili powder and cayenne pepper. Cook until the beans are warmed through and softened, stirring often, about 5 to 7 minutes. If the beans seem dry at any point, mix in a little splash of water.
- To serve, spoon generous portions of rice, beans and kale salad into a bowl along with a couple spoonfuls of avocado salsa verde. Garnish with chopped cherry tomatoes.

Per Serving: Calories: 494; Total Fat: 17g; Saturated Fat: 2g; Protein: 17g; Carbs: 82g; Fiber: 21g; Sugar: 3g

Cowboy Caviar

Serves: 4 / Preparation time: 15 minutes / Cooking time: 15 minutes

Cowboy caviar

2 (14-ounce) cans black-eyed peas, rinsed and drained, or 3 cups cooked black-eyed peas

1 (14-ounce) can black beans, rinsed and drained, or 1 ½ cups cooked black beans

1 ½ cups fresh corn kernels (about 2 ears of corn), or 1 (14-ounce) can corn, drained

1 ½ cups chopped tomatoes (I used about 4 Roma tomatoes, about ¾ pound)

1 medium red, orange or yellow bell pepper

¾ cup chopped red onion (about ½ small red onion)

½ cup chopped cilantro, leaves and stems

1 to 2 jalapeños, ribs removed, seeded and finely chopped

1 avocado (optional)

Italian dressing

⅓ cup olive oil

3 tablespoons red wine vinegar or lime juice

2 medium cloves garlic, pressed or minced

1 to 1 ½ teaspoons salt, to taste

1 teaspoon dried oregano

½ teaspoon dried basil

1 teaspoon maple syrup or honey

⅛ teaspoon red pepper flakes

Freshly ground black pepper, to taste

- In a large serving bowl, combine the drained black-eyed peas, black beans, corn, chopped tomatoes, bell pepper, onion, cilantro and jalapeño. If you'll be including avocado, wait to dice it until you're ready to serve the dip, so it doesn't turn brown in the meantime.
- In a cup, whisk together the dressing ingredients until emulsified. Drizzle the dressing over the serving bowl and toss until well mixed. Season to taste with additional salt and pepper. For best flavor, let the mixture marinate for at least 20 minutes before serving. If you're adding avocado, mix it in just before serving.

Per Serving: Calories: 142; Total Fat: 4g; Saturated Fat: 1g; Protein: 5g; Carbs: 21g; Fiber: 6g; Sugar: 1g

GRAINS

Contents

Mushroom and Kale Farro Salad

Serves: 4 / Preparation time: 5 minutes / Cooking time: 5 minutes

1 1/2 cups farro

1 small red onion

1/4 cup vegetable broth

1 garlic clove, minced

2 cups mushrooms, chopped

3 cups kale, torn into small pieces

2 tablespoons tamari

2 tablespoons chopped parsley

Salt and pepper, to taste

1/4 cup pomegranate seeds

1/4 cup pumpkin seeds

- Boil the farro according to directions on the package. Drain and transfer to large bowl and set aside.
- In a separate medium-sized pan, heat the vegetable broth until hot and start sautéing the onions, adding in the garlic 2-3 minutes after. Stir in the mushrooms, kale, tamari, parsley, salt, and pepper, adding in extra vegetable broth if needed. Cook until mushrooms are soft, about 5 minutes. Turn off heat.
- Transfer the vegetables and any extra liquid in the pan to the bowl with the farro and mix. Fold in the pomegranate and pumpkin seeds. Serve warm or at room temperature.

Per Serving: Calories: 122; Total Fat: 3g; Saturated Fat: 1g; Protein: 8g; Carbs: 21g; Fiber: 4g; Sugar: 1g

Rainbow Chard Wraps With Millet and Chickpeas

Serves: 4 / Preparation time: 5 minutes / Cooking time: 10 minutes

1/2 cup uncooked millet

1/2 cup chickpeas, cooked

1 bunch rainbow swiss chard

1 carrot, shaved into ribbons

1/2 english cucumber, shaved into ribbons

1 cup sliced cabbage

1/3 cup hummus

Fresh mint leaves

Sprinkle of hemp seeds

- Cook the millet according to package directions and set aside the cooked or canned chickpeas.
- Rinse and dry the swiss chard and chop off the stem. Shave the woody part off of the bottom stem, making it thinner, to make rolling easier.
- Chop and julienne the carrots, cucumber, and cabbage. Set aside.
- To assemble, top the center of each chard leaf with hummus. Add a spoonful of cooked millet followed by sliced carrots, cucumber, and cabbage. Add a spoonful of cooked chickpeas, a sprinkle of hemp seeds and a few fresh mint leaves to finish up.
- Wrap up like a burrito and serve.

Per Serving: Calories: 369; Total Fat: 7g; Saturated Fat: 1g; Protein: 11g; Carbs: 44g; Fiber: 12g; Sugar: 3g

Vegetable Paella Risotto

Serves: 4 / Preparation time: 5 minutes / Cooking time: 15 minutes

1 tablespoon olive oil

1/2 onion, diced

4 garlic cloves, chopped

1 cup Arborio rice

1 teaspoon smoked paprika

1 1/2 tablespoons tomato paste

1 packet saffron seasoning or a generous pinch saffron

1 cup frozen peas

3 carrots, cut into strips

1/2 red bell pepper, cut into strips

6-8 asparagus spears

3 cups vegetable broth

4 cups water

Salt and pepper, to taste

Lemon and parsley, for garnish

- Preheat oven to 375°F.
- Roast carrots, red bell pepper, and asparagus for 15 minutes. Remove and let cool.
- Place your vegetable broth and water into a small pot and heat until it just begins to simmer. Remove from heat and keep close to the pan you will use for the rice.
- In a larger pot/pan, sweat onion and garlic together with olive oil until onion begins to turn translucent. Add tomato paste, saffron packet, and smoked paprika. Stir around and then add rice. Stir rice to soak up oil and seasonings.
- Begin to add broth/water mixture 1 cup at a time. After each addition, stir the rice until most of the liquid is soaked up. Then, add 1 more cup. Continue to do this until all water is used or rice is cooked.
- Top risotto with vegetables, lemon, and parsley and serve warm.

Per Serving: Calories: 145; Total Fat: 5g; Saturated Fat: 1g; Protein: 3g; Carbs: 24g; Fiber: 4g; Sugar: 4g

Quinoa Bread

Serves: 4 / Preparation time: 15 minutes / Cooking time: 15 minutes

1 1/2 cups quinoa

2 cups, plus 1 3/4 tablespoons water

3 tablespoons chia seeds

1/3 cup, plus 1 1/2 tablespoons water

1 teaspoon salt

3 tablespoons, plus 1 teaspoon olive oil

2 teaspoons baking powder

2 tablespoons vinegar

1 tablespoon agave nectar or maple syrup

- Preheat oven to 390°F.
- Pour 1/3 cup, plus 1 1/2 tablespoons water over chia seeds. Let stand for 25-30 minutes until a gel forms.
- Cook the quinoa in 2 cups, plus 1 3/4 tablespoons water with 1 teaspoon salt on low heat for 15-17 minutes or until quinoa has absorbed all the water.
- Blend in a food processor quinoa, chia gel, oil, baking powder, vinegar, and sweetener.
- Transfer the mix to an oven dish or silicone mould. Bread can easily jump out of it. Put the dish in the oven and bake the bread for one hour. Allow to cool. It will take approximately an hour. Be patient and make really sure to let it cool thoroughly before cutting into slices.

Per Serving: Calories: 83; Total Fat: 2g; Saturated Fat: 1g; Protein: 4g; Carbs: 14g; Fiber: 2g; Sugar: 3g

Asian-Style Rice Crust Pizza With Mushrooms

Serves: 4 / Preparation time: 15 minutes / Cooking time: 15 minutes

For the Crust:

1 1/2 cup uncooked short grain rice

2 1/2 cup water

1 teaspoon sugar (optional)

1 tablespoon chili flakes (optional)

1/2 teaspoon garlic powder (optional)

For the Sauce:

1/2 cup tomato passata or tomato purée

1 teaspoon soy sauce

1/4 teaspoon ginger

1 tablespoon chili flakes

1 tablespoon nutritional yeast

1/4 teaspoon garlic and onion powder

For the Toppings:

2 1/2 cups oyster mushrooms

1 teaspoon soy sauce

1 teaspoon sugar

2 scallions

1 chili pepper

Baby corn

- Wash and rinse the rice about four times. Bring the rice to a boil with about 2 1/2 cups of water. Once the water starts to boil, turn down the heat, cover the pot, and let it simmer for about 12 minutes. Turn off the heat and place the rice in a bowl. Add the garlic powder, chili flakes, and sugar to the rice and mix well. Let it cool down before making the crust.
- Preheat your oven to 350°F. Place the rice on a piece of parchment paper, wet your hands and shape the rice into the shape of a pizza. Place the crust in the oven and cook it for about 20 minutes. Prepare the toppings while it cooks.
- After about 35 minutes, remove the crust from the oven, add a layer of tomato sauce, and add the toppings. Bake for 15 more minutes.
- Slice and serve.

Per Serving: Calories: 83; Total Fat: 2g; Saturated Fat: 1g; Protein: 4g; Carbs: 14g; Fiber: 2g; Sugar: 3g

Teff Porridge With Blood Orange and Coconut Butter

Serves: 4 / Preparation time: 5 minutes / Cooking time: 15 minutes

1/2 cup plus 1 tablespoon almond milk

2 tablespoons teff grain

A tiny pinch of sea salt

1-2 teaspoons coconut butter

1 teaspoon maple syrup

1/8 teaspoon ground cardamom

1/2 teaspoon maca or lucuma

1-2 teaspoon hemp seeds

1 blood orange

- Heat the almond milk in a small saucepan over medium-high heat. When the milk just starts to boil, stir in the teff and salt and turn the heat to low. Simmer the teff porridge for 10-15 minutes until it has thickened.
- Stir in the coconut butter, syrup, cardamom, and maca. Once the coconut butter has melted completely, remove the porridge from the heat. Serve warm.

Per Serving: Calories: 190; Total Fat: 9g; Saturated Fat: 4g; Protein: 7g; Carbs: 44g; Fiber: 7g; Sugar: 17g

Chickpea and Edamame Quinoa Salad

Serves: 4 / Preparation time: 15 minutes / Cooking time: 20 minutes

1 cup uncooked quinoa

2 cups water

1 cup edamame, cooked and shelled

1/3 cup sliced almonds

1 15-ounce can chickpeas, rinsed and drained

1 cup Italian parsley, finely chopped

1/3 cup dried cranberries

1 red bell pepper, diced

2 tablespoons extra virgin olive oil

1 lime, juiced

2 teaspoons balsamic vinegar

1/2 teaspoon Kosher salt

Fresh cracked pepper, to taste

- In a medium-sized pot over medium heat, combine the quinoa and the water. Bring the mixture to a gentle boil, then cover the pot and reduce heat to a simmer and cook for 15 minutes.
- Remove the quinoa from heat and let it rest, still covered, for 5 minutes. Add the quinoa to a large bowl, fluff with a fork, and set it aside to cool.
- Meanwhile, cook the edamame according to the package directions.
- To toast the sliced almonds, heat them in a small skillet over medium-low heat, stirring frequently, until they are fragrant and begin to turn golden on the edges.
- Transfer toasted almonds to the same bowl that the quinoa is in. Add in the chickpeas, chopped parsley, dried cranberries, and diced bell pepper. Toss to combine.
- Mix together the dressing ingredients (olive oil, lime juice, balsamic, salt, and pepper) in a small jar and adjust to taste, if necessary.
- Drizzle the dressing over the quinoa salad, add salt to taste, and chill until ready to serve.

Per Serving: Calories: 236; Total Fat: 10g; Saturated Fat: 1g; Protein: 9g; Carbs: 29g; Fiber: 3g; Sugar: 3g

Carrot Barley Risotto

Serves: 4 / Preparation time: 5 minutes / Cooking time: 60 minutes

1/2 cup whole barley	1 little carrot
1 teaspoon extra virgin olive oil	A sprinkle of orange zest
1 teaspoon grated ginger	A few fresh thyme leaves
1 teaspoon grated garlic	A small handful of almond flakes
Warm vegetable broth, as much as needed	

- Soak the barley for 24 hours.
- Rinse, drain, and set aside.
- Heat the oil in a little pot, add ginger and garlic, and cook over medium heat, stirring to prevent burning.
- Add barley, stir for one minute at high flame, cover with warm broth, and let cook at low flame for about 1 hour, half adding more broth when needed.
- In the meantime add the chopped carrots to the broth. When it's tender, blend with the broth until smooth, and add the purée to barley.
- When barley is tender, add more broth if needed. Serve, sprinkle with orange zest, thyme leaves, and almond flakes.

Per Serving: Calories: 201; Total Fat: 5g; Saturated Fat: 1g; Protein: 6g; Carbs: 31g; Fiber: 5g; Sugar: 1g

Baked Zucchini and Amaranth Patties

Serves: 4 / Preparation time: 5 minutes / Cooking time: 20 minutes

1/2 cup amaranth seeds

1 1/2 cups vegetable broth

1 1/2 cups shredded zucchini

1/2 shredded onion

1 15-ounce can white beans (cannellini or great northern), or 1 1/2 cups cooked

1 tablespoon salsa

1 teaspoon chili powder

1/2 teaspoon cumin

1/2 cup cornmeal or breadcrumbs (gluten-free, if necessary)

1/4 cup flax meal

- Preheat oven to 400°F. Line a baking sheet with parchment paper and set aside.
- In a pot on the stove, place the amaranth and vegetable stock. Bring to a boil, then reduce the heat to simmer, uncovered, until the water is absorbed.
- Meanwhile, place white beans in a large bowl and smash with a potato masher or fork until mostly broken down (a few whole beans left is fine).
- Add all remaining ingredients to the white beans, including the amaranth once it's cooked and cooled enough to handle. Mix well.
- Form into patties and place onto the parchment lined baking sheet.
- Bake 20 minutes, flip the patties over and bake another 10 minutes, until crispy on both sides.
- Serve with salsa and vegan sour cream, if using.

Per Serving: Calories: 152; Total Fat: 3g; Saturated Fat: 1g; Protein: 6g; Carbs: 31g; Fiber: 6g; Sugar: 1g

Cheesy Quinoa Meatballs

Serves: 4 / Preparation time: 10 minutes / Cooking time: 20 minutes

1 cup quinoa, rinsed and drained

1 tablespoon flax meal

3 tablespoons water

2 tablespoons olive oil, divided in 2

1 cup yellow onion, finely diced

3 garlic cloves, minced

1 teaspoon dried basil

1 teaspoon dried oregano

1 teaspoon paprika

1/2 teaspoon salt

1 teaspoon lemon zest

1 cup vegan mozzarella, grated and chopped

Marinara sauce, for serving

Fresh parsley, for garnish (optional)

- Cook quinoa according to package instructions. Transfer to a bowl and set aside.
- In a small bowl, combine flax seed meal and water and stir to combine. Set aside.
- In a large sauté pan, heat 1 tablespoon of olive oil. Add onion and sauté for 1-2 minutes. Stir in garlic, dried basil, dried oregano, paprika, and salt. Stir in cooked quinoa and mix well, cooking another minute or two. Transfer quinoa mixture to a large bowl.
- Stir in flax seed "egg," lemon zest, and non-dairy cheese shreds and mix well.
- Form quinoa into balls about 1 1/2-inches in diameter. Place on a lined baking sheet. You should end up with about 12. Refrigerate quinoa meatballs for 30 minutes.
- Preheat oven to 400°F.
- Brush quinoa meatballs with remaining tablespoon of olive oil. Bake about 20 minutes until brown.
- When serving, top with marinara sauce and fresh parsley, if you'd like.

Per Serving: Calories: 240; Total Fat: 8g; Saturated Fat: 1g; Protein: 16g; Carbs: 31g; Fiber: 3g; Sugar: 0.1g

Cheesy Rice Stuffed Jalapeños

Serves: 4 / Preparation time: 10 minutes / Cooking time: 20 minutes

3 medium-sized potatoes, cubed

2 long carrots, chopped

3 tablespoons water or oil

1/2 cup nutritional yeast

1-2 teaspoons salt

1/4 teaspoon onion powder

1/4 teaspoon garlic powder

Juice of 1 lime

Cooked rice

3 whole jalapeños, halved

1 red bell pepper, sliced, for garnish

- Preheat oven to 400°F.
- Boil or steam 2 cups of peeled and chopped potatoes and 1 cup chopped carrots
- Once soft, put cooked vegetables in blender with 1/2 cup of water, then blend until smooth
- Add 1-2 teaspoons salt, 1/4 teaspoon garlic powder, 1/4 teaspoon onion powder, and juice from the lime.
- Add either 3 tablespoons of oil or water, then blend until smooth.
- Add 1/2 cup nutritional yeast flakes and blend. Add tiny amounts of water if it's too thick to blend.
- Halve the jalapeños and brush them with oil and salt, if desired. Mix cheese sauce with cooked rice and stuff in a jalapeño.
- Top with sliced red bell pepper, if using.
- Bake at 400°F for 20 minutes.

Per Serving: Calories: 150; Total Fat: 12g; Saturated Fat: 7g; Protein: 8g; Carbs: 2g; Fiber: 1g; Sugar: 1g

Carrot Poppyseed Buckwheat Porridge

Serves: 4 / Preparation time: 30 minutes / Cooking time: 15 minutes

1/2 cup buckwheat groats

2 teaspoons cinnamon

1/2 teaspoon nutmeg

2 tablespoons hemp hearts

1 cup water

1 cup coconut milk

1 teaspoon coconut nectar

1 teaspoon vanilla extract

1/4 cup grated carrot

2 tablespoons poppy seeds

- Begin by placing buckwheat groats and water in a medium saucepan and allowing the groats soak for 30-60 minutes, or overnight.
- After soaking, add all of the remaining ingredients except for the carrots and poppy seeds, and stir together.
- Cook over medium heat, stirring often, until nearly cooked, and most of the liquid has evaporated.
- In the last 10 minutes of cooking, add in carrots and poppy seeds and finish cooking.
- Serve garnished with raisins, nuts or anything else you choose.

Per Serving: Calories: 330; Total Fat: 5g; Saturated Fat: 3g; Protein: 11g; Carbs: 30g; Fiber: 8g; Sugar: 1g

Fermented Buckwheat Bread

Serves: 4 / Preparation time: 10 minutes / Cooking time: 15 minutes

2 1/2 cups raw buckwheat groats

1 1/4 cups water, plus water for soaking buckwheat

2 tablespoons agave nectar

1/2-1 teaspoon sea salt

2 tablespoons oregano

3 handfuls of sunflower seeds

- Soak buckwheat groats for at least 6 hours. Rinse well and let drain for 2-5 minutes.
- Place drained buckwheat groats into blender with 1 1/4 cups of water. Blend on low speed until smooth batter forms.
- Pour the batter into plastic or glass bowl (do not use a metal bowl). Cover the bowl with clean cloth and place into a warm oven, about 85°F.
- Let the batter ferment for 7 hours.
- After 7 hours you'll see that the batter has risen and small bubbles have formed. If you don't see that, let it ferment a bit longer.
- Now, add all the other ingredients to this buckwheat bread recipe, gently and briefly stir with a wooden or plastic spoon (do not use a metal spoon). Do not over-mix as the batter will lose its fluffiness.
- Pour the batter into a loaf pan lined with parchment paper. Now, you can put the bread back into the warm oven and let it rise for another few hours or you can bake it immediately for 1 hour at 350°F. If you used parchment paper, remove the bread from pan immediately and place on about 3-4 pieces of folded paper towel, which will absorb the excess moisture. Let the bread cool for an hour before slicing.

Per Serving: Calories: 82; Total Fat: 1g; Saturated Fat: 0.1g; Protein: 3g; Carbs: 14g; Fiber: 3g; Sugar: 1g

Mexican Cornbread Pizza Cake

Serves: 4 / Preparation time: 10 minutes / Cooking time: 90 minutes

For the Cake:
1/2 of 1 15.5-ounce can oil-free refried beans
3/4 cup guacamole
1/3 cup vegan nacho cheese
Pizza sauce of your choice
Sliced avocado
Grilled bell peppers
Diced red onion
Fire-roasted corn
3 batches of the sun-dried tomato jalapeño lime cornbread (recipe below)
For the Sun-Dried Tomato Jalapeño Lime Cornbread:

1 1/2 cups cornmeal
1/3 cup applesauce
1 tablespoon chia seeds
3 tablespoons water
1 cup unsweetened almond milk
1 tablespoon apple cider vinegar
3 teaspoons baking powder
1/2 teaspoon salt
Oil, for the skillet
2 tablespoons jalapeños, diced plus more to top if desired
2-3 tablespoons salt-free sun-dried tomatoes, roughly chopped
2 tablespoons maple syrup

- To Make the Cornbread:
- Preheat oven to 425°F and line a circular baking pan with parchment paper.
- Whisk together chia seeds and water in a small bowl. Set aside to thicken and create a chia egg.
- Add apple cider vinegar to milk and set aside for about 5 minutes.
- In a large bowl add cornmeal, baking powder, salt, and combine thoroughly. Add in the sun-dried tomatoes and jalapeños, then mix again.
- Add applesauce, milk mixture, and chia egg to dry ingredients. Mix just to combine.
- Pour cornbread into baking pan, filling it to the top. Bake for about 15 minutes until the edges brown and a toothpick comes out clean.
- To Make the Pizza Cake:
- Top the first layer of the cornbread with refried beans and nacho cheese. Add the next layer on top of that, then top with guacamole. Add the final layer, then top with pizza sauce, sliced avocado, grilled bell peppers, diced red onion, and fire-roasted corn.
- Serve sliced with a side of lime.

Per Serving: Calories: 170; Total Fat: 6g; Saturated Fat: 2g; Protein: 5g; Carbs: 25g; Fiber: 1g; Sugar: 3g

Sweet and Sour Pineapple Sticky Rice

Serves: 4 / Preparation time: 10 minutes / Cooking time: 15 minutes

1 medium-sized sweet potato, diced

2 cups fresh pineapple, diced

kernels of one corn cob

1 red bell pepper, sliced

1 tablespoon extra virgin olive oil

2 tablespoons coconut sugar

2 tablespoons ketchup

1 tablespoon tamari soy sauce

2 tablespoons apple cider vinegar

Juice of 1/2 a lemon

1 tablespoon Sriracha (optional)

2 cups cooked brown rice

- Start by heating the olive oil to medium heat. Add the diced sweet potato and cook over medium heat for about 10 minutes, stirring occasionally. Add the pineapple, red bell pepper and corn kernels, stir well to combine and keep cooking for additional 10-15 minutes.
- Add the coconut sugar, ketchup, tamari soy sauce, apple cider vinegar, and lemon juice, then stir well to combine. Let simmer covered for about five minutes. Add the brown rice and stir well combine. Serve with some fresh lime.

Per Serving: Calories: 170; Total Fat: 6g; Saturated Fat: 2g; Protein: 5g; Carbs: 25g; Fiber: 1g; Sugar: 3g

One-Pan Cheesy Mexican Quinoa

Serves: 4 / Preparation time: 10 minutes / Cooking time: 45 minutes

2 teaspoons olive oil

1 cup red pepper, finely chopped

1/2 cup onion, finely chopped

1 tablespoon fresh garlic, minced

1 1/3 cups reduced-sodium vegetable broth

1 cup frozen corn kernels

2/3 cup salsa, of choice

2/3 cup chickpeas, drained and rinsed

1/2 cup black beans, drained and rinsed

1/2 cup nutritional yeast

1/2 tablespoon ground cumin

1/4 teaspoon salt

Pepper

1 cup quinoa, uncooked

Cilantro, for garnish

- Preheat your oven to 350°F.
- Heat the oil in a 12-inch sauté pan on medium heat.
- Add the pepper, onion, and garlic, and cook until lightly golden brown, stirring frequently.
- Into the pan, add the broth, frozen corn, salsa, chickpeas, black beans, nutritional yeast, cumin, salt, and a pinch of pepper, and stir well.
- Stir in the quinoa until all the grains are incorporated into the liquid. Bring the mixture to a boil.
- Once boiling, cover the pan and place it into the oven. Cook until the quinoa has absorbed all of the liquid, about 40-45 minutes.
- Garnish with cilantro and serve.

Per Serving: Calories: 306; Total Fat: 6g; Saturated Fat: 1g; Protein: 12g; Carbs: 54g; Fiber: 13g; Sugar: 1g

Sorghum Banana Paniyaram

Serves: 4 / Preparation time: 10 minutes / Cooking time: 15 minutes

3/4 cup sorghum

2 tablespoons rice flour

3/4 cup grated palm jaggery

1 medium sized banana, mashed

1 teaspoon cardamom powder

1 teaspoon baking powder

- Wash and soak sorghum in water overnight. After draining the water completely, blend in a mixer until a smooth paste, adding 2-3 tablespoons water. Transfer to a mixing bowl.
- Add rice flour, baking powder, grated jaggery, cardamom powder, and mashed banana. Mix everything well with a spoon. Add water until the mixture reaches a pouring consistency, it should not be too thick or too watery. Keep mixture aside for 10 minutes.
- Heat a paniyaram pan and grease with oil. Pour a spoonful of prepared batter in all the cups of pan. Fry paniyaram evenly on both the sides by rotating the buns with a needle-like wooden stick. Cook on low-medium flame until it turns golden brown on both the sides. Serve hot.

Per Serving: Calories: 325; Total Fat: 3g; Saturated Fat: 1g; Protein: 10g; Carbs: 70g; Fiber: 0g; Sugar: 0g

Zucchini Waffles

Serves: 4 / Preparation time: 10 minutes / Cooking time: 15 minutes

14 ounces zucchini

3 cups einkorn flour

5 tablespoons vegan butter

2 chia eggs (2 tablespoons ground chia seeds, plus 6 tablespoons water)

2 teaspoons baking powder

1 teaspoon salt

2 cups rice milk

1/2 ounce basil

Oil, to grease waffle maker

Tomatoes, to garnish

- Make chia eggs by mixing in a bowl 2 tablespoons ground chia seeds with 6 tablespoons water. Set aside.
- Grate zucchini with the coarse side of a cheese grater.
- Melt butter in a small saucepan.
- In the bowl of a food processor, mix together einkorn flour, baking powder, and salt.
- Mix melted butter with flour. Carry on mixing while adding chia eggs followed by rice milk. The mixture should be well blended.
- Add grated zucchini and chopped basil. Blend until everything is well mixed together and there are no lumps.
- Preheat the waffle maker brushed with vegetable oil.
- Pour waffle batter, one ladle at a time, into the waffle maker. Cook each waffle for around 4-5 minutes until golden and crispy.
- Serve hot with chopped tomatoes on top. Don't forget to oil the waffle maker with vegetable oil between each waffle.

Per Serving: Calories: 273; Total Fat: 12g; Saturated Fat: 6g; Protein: 18g; Carbs: 19g; Fiber: 1g; Sugar: 2g

Summer Berry Spelt Buns

Serves: 4 / Preparation time: 10 minutes / Cooking time: 25 minutes

For the Dough:
1 tablespoon active dry yeast
1/3 cup pure maple syrup
1/4 cup coconut oil
3/4 cup non-dairy milk of choice, lukewarm
or at room temperature
1 1/2 tablespoon flax meal
1/2 teaspoon fine sea salt
2 1/2 cups spelt flour, plus extra for dusting

For the Filling:
3 cups mixed berries (blueberries, black
currants, raspberries, blackberries, etc.)
1/4 cup pure maple syrup
1 teaspoon ground cardamom
1/2 teaspoon pure vanilla extract
Zest of 1 orange
For the Glaze:
1 tablespoon pure maple syrup
1 tablespoon freshly squeezed orange juice

- To Make the Dough:
- Place maple syrup in a small bowl and sprinkle yeast on top. If you keep your maple syrup in the refrigerator or freezer, bring it to room temp first or warm it through on the
- Place maple syrup in a small bowl and sprinkle yeast on top. If you keep your maple syrup in the refrigerator or freezer, bring it to room temp first or warm it through on the
- Place maple syrup in a small bowl and sprinkle yeast on top. If you keep your maple syrup in the refrigerator or freezer, bring it to room temp first or warm it through on the stovetop. Set aside. Melt coconut oil in a small saucepan and place over low heat. Swirl the pot as the oil melts to keep it from getting too hot. Once the oil is fully melted, remove from heat and let cool. Add flax meal, salt, and non-dairy milk to a large bowl, then whisk to combine. Whisk in cooled, yet still liquid, coconut oil and then maple yeast mixture. Whisk to combine ingredients.
- Sift in flour 1/2 cup at a time, stirring with a wooden spoon or spatula in between. Stir in enough flour to make a firm but sticky dough. Then, turn onto a floured surface and knead, adding more flour until the dough is smooth and elastic. You might need more or less flour, up to 3 cups. Form a ball with the dough and place in an oiled bowl and flip the dough to coat in oil. Cover with a dry tea towel and let rise in a warm place until doubled in size, about 1 1/2 to 2 hours, up to 3 hours.
- To Make the Filling:
- When the dough is ready, combine all the filling ingredients in a large bowl and mix gently with your fingertips, being careful not to mush up the berries too much.

- To Make the Rolls:
- Punch down the dough on a lightly floured surface, and knead until smooth. Roll the dough out into a large rectangle, then spread over the berries and their juices, leaving a bit of space around the edges. Roll up from the long side, tucking the berries in as you go, once you get close to the edge, pull the long side of the dough up onto the roll to get everything inside. You may
- Cut into slices and place in an oiled pan leaving space between the pieces. Cover and let rise until doubled in size, about another hour. Preheat oven to 350°F and bake for 20-25 minutes, or until golden on top and firm to the touch. Let cool.
- To Make the Glaze:
- Mix maple syrup and orange juice in small bowl and brush over the top of the slightly cooled buns. Top with extra orange zest.

Per Serving: Calories: 193; Total Fat: 6g; Saturated Fat: 0.1g; Protein: 4g; Carbs: 33g; Fiber: 2g; Sugar: 4g

Rosemary Garlic Spelt Agnolotti

Serves: 4 / Preparation time: 10 minutes / Cooking time: 25 minutes

For the Pasta Dough:
2 tablespoons ground flaxseed, plus 3 tablespoons warm water
2 tablespoons extra virgin olive oil
2 cups spelt flour
1/2 cup water
1/2 teaspoon sea salt
1/2 teaspoon black pepper
A bit more flour, for rolling
A bit of olive oil, for assembly
For the Rosemary Garlic Cannellini Filling:
2 cups cannellini beans, cooked

3 cloves garlic, minced
1/2 tablespoons fresh rosemary, minced
1/2 tablespoons dried chives
2 tablespoons extra virgin olive oil
A pinch of sea salt and pepper
For the Mesclun Pesto:
1 cup arugula
1 1/2 cups mesclun greens
1/4 cup extra virgin olive oil
1 tablespoon white wine vinegar
A pinch of sea salt and pepper

- **To Make the Dough:**
- In a small bowl, combine ground flaxseed and warm water. Mix completely and let sit while you prepare the rest of the dough ingredients. By the time you add the flax mixture to the dough, the texture should be sticky and gelatinous. If it's not, let it rest for a few more minutes.
- In a larger bowl, combine flour, sea salt, and pepper. Whisk together.
- Then, add olive oil, giving flour another whisk to mix completely.
- After the olive oil has been mixed, add in flaxseed mixture and combine.
- Finally, add in the water and mix.
- If the dough is too dry, add water in small increments until it is workable but still firm.
- If you have a stand mixer with a kneading attachment, use that. Otherwise, knead the dough for a good 3-4 minutes. Afterwards, let the dough rest while you prepare the filling.
- To Make the Rosemary Garlic Cannellini Filling:
- In a food processor, combine beans, minced garlic, minced rosemary, dried chives, olive oil, salt, and pepper. Process until beans are a smooth, creamy texture. Taste and adjust seasonings as needed.

- **To Make the Agnolotti:**
- When you're ready to make your agnolotti, take the dough and separate it into about four parts. This number doesn't really matter — you're just using smaller amounts to help you roll the pasta.
- If you have a pasta-rolling extension on your stand mixer, go ahead and use it. Otherwise, use a rolling pin.
- On a clean, well-floured surface, roll your dough out until it is fairly thin.
- To get the round agnolotti shape, take a standard size mason jar lid or a similarly-sized glass and cut out your shapes. A cookie cutter would probably work too.
- When you've cut as many circles as you can out of the dough you've rolled, repeat the process with the remaining dough. Save the dough you have leftover from each repetition, and at the end, add a little water to reconstitute the dough, and roll it out again so nothing is wasted!
- To make your agnolotti, scoop about a scant 1/2 tablespoon of the filling in the middle of your little pasta circle. Using a clean paintbrush or your finger, dab a little olive oil around the circumference of the circle.
- Fold circle in half over the filling. Using a fork, press the tips of the fork down on the edges of the half-circle, to "seal" the agnolotti.
- To Cook the Agnolotti:
- To cook the agnolotti, bring a pot of well-salted water to boil.
- Taking about 8-10 agnolotti at a time, place in boiling water. They are done cooking when they float to the surface.
- Repeat for as many agnolotti as you'd like to serve.
- This step is optional but recommended. Bring a pan and a little olive oil to medium heat. When pan is hot, add a few agnolotti and cook until browned on each side, about 2-3 minutes. This really adds a lot to the texture.
- To Make the Mesclun Pesto:
- In a food processor, combine all pesto ingredients and pulse until desired consistency is reached. Adjust seasonings if needed.
- To Serve:
- To serve, take agnolotti hot from the pan and drizzle with pesto. Serve with chopped herbs or extra chopped mesclun greens, if desired.

Per Serving: Calories: 120; Total Fat: 1g; Saturated Fat: 0.1g; Protein: 5g; Carbs: 24g; Fiber: 20g; Sugar: 4g

VEGETABLES

Contents

Sugar Snap Pea and Carrot Soba Noodles

Serves: 4 / Preparation time: 25 minutes / Cooking time: 5 minutes

Soba

6 ounces soba noodles or spaghetti noodles of choice

2 cups frozen organic edamame

10 ounces (about 3 cups) sugar snap peas or snow peas

6 medium-sized carrots, peeled

½ cup chopped fresh cilantro (about 2 handfuls)

¼ cup sesame seeds

Ginger-sesame sauce

¼ cup reduced-sodium tamari or soy sauce

2 tablespoons quality peanut oil or extra-virgin olive oil

1 small lime, juiced

1 tablespoon toasted sesame oil

1 tablespoon honey or agave nectar

1 tablespoon white miso*

2 teaspoons freshly grated ginger

1 teaspoon chili garlic sauce or sriracha

- To prepare the vegetables: Use a chef's knife to slice the peas in half lengthwise (or just roughly chop them). Slice the carrots into long, thin strips with a julienne peeler, or slice them into ribbons with a vegetable peeler.
- To make the sauce: whisk together the ingredients in a small bowl until emulsified. Set aside.
- Bring two big pots of water to a boil. In the meantime, toast the sesame seeds: Pour the sesame seeds into a small pan. Toast for about 4 to 5 minutes over medium-low heat, shaking the pan frequently to prevent burning, until the seeds are turning golden and starting to make popping noises.
- Once the pots of water are boiling: In one pot, cook the soba noodles just until al dente, according to package directions (probably about 5 minutes), then drain and briefly rinse under cool water. Cook the frozen edamame in the other pot until warmed through (about 4 to 6 minutes) but before draining, toss the halved peas into the boiling edamame water and cook for an additional 20 seconds. Drain.
- Combine the soba noodles, edamame, snap peas and carrots in a large serving bowl. Pour in the dressing and toss with salad servers. Toss in the chopped cilantro and toasted sesame seeds. Serve.

Per Serving: Calories: 362; Total Fat: 13g; Saturated Fat: 2g; Protein: 17g; Carbs: 53g; Fiber: 6g; Sugar: 7g

Vegetable Paella

Serves: 4 / Preparation time: 15 minutes / Cooking time: 60 minutes

3 tablespoons extra-virgin olive oil, divided

1 medium yellow onion, chopped fine

1 ½ teaspoons fine sea salt, divided

6 garlic cloves, pressed or minced

2 teaspoons smoked paprika

1 can (15 ounces) diced tomatoes (preferably the fire-roasted variety), drained

2 cups short-grain brown rice

1 can (15 ounces) chickpeas, rinsed and drained, or 1 ½ cups cooked chickpeas

3 cups vegetable broth

⅓ cup dry white wine or vegetable broth

½ teaspoon saffron threads, crumbled (optional)

1 can (14 ounces) quartered artichokes or 1 jar (12 ounces) marinated artichoke, drained

2 red bell peppers, stemmed, seeded and sliced into long, ½"-wide strips

½ cup Kalamata olives, pitted and halved

Freshly ground black pepper

¼ cup chopped fresh parsley, plus about 1 tablespoon more for garnish

2 tablespoons lemon juice, plus additional lemon wedges for garnish

½ cup frozen peas

- Arrange your oven racks in the upper and lower thirds of the oven, making sure that you have ample space between the two racks for your Dutch oven. You're going to need a large Dutch oven (preferably 6 quarts/11-to-12" in diameter or bigger, although I got by with my 5.5-quart Le Creuset) or a large skillet with a snug-fitting lid (both must be oven-safe!).

- Preheat the oven to 350 degrees Fahrenheit. Heat 2 tablespoons of the oil in your Dutch oven or skillet over medium heat until shimmering. Add the onion and a pinch of salt. Cook until the onions are tender and translucent, about 5 minutes.

- Stir in the garlic and paprika and cook until fragrant, about 30 seconds. Stir in the tomatoes and cook until the mixture begins to darken and thicken slightly, about 2 minutes Stir in the rice and cook until the grains are well coated with tomato mixture, about 1 minute. Stir in the chickpeas, broth, wine, saffron (if using) and 1 teaspoon salt.

- Increase the heat to medium-high and bring the mixture to a boil, stirring occasionally. Cover the pot and transfer it to the lower rack in the oven. Bake, undisturbed, until the liquid is absorbed and the rice is tender, 50 to 55 minutes.

- Meanwhile, line a large, rimmed baking sheet with parchment paper for easy cleanup. On the baking sheet, combine the artichoke, peppers, chopped olives, 1 tablespoon of the olive oil, ½ teaspoon of the salt, and about 10 twists of freshly ground black pepper. Toss to combine, then spread the contents evenly across the pan.

- Roast the vegetables on the upper rack until the artichokes and peppers are tender and browned around the edges, about 40 to 45 minutes. Remove from the oven and let the vegetables cool for a few minutes. Add ¼ cup parsley to the pan and the lemon juice, and toss to combine. Season with salt and pepper, to taste. Set aside.

- For optional socarrat (crispy bottom—beware that you might have to scrub burnt bits from your pot later if you do this): Uncover the pot of baked rice, transfer it to the stovetop and cook over medium-high heat for about 5 minutes, rotating the pot as needed, until the bottom layer of rice is well browned and crisp.

- Socarrat or not, sprinkle the peas and roasted vegetables over the baked rice, cover, and let the paella sit for 5 minutes. Garnish with a sprinkle of chopped parsley (about 1 tablespoon) and serve in individual bowls, with lemon wedges on the side.

Per Serving: Calories: 362; Total Fat: 13g; Saturated Fat: 2g; Protein: 17g; Carbs: 53g; Fiber: 6g; Sugar: 7g

Spaghetti Squash Burrito Bowls

Serves: 4 / Preparation time: 10 minutes / Cooking time: 15 minutes

Roasted spaghetti squash
2 medium spaghetti squash (about 2 pounds each), halved and seeds removed
2 tablespoons olive oil
Salt and freshly ground black pepper
Cabbage and black bean slaw
2 cups purple cabbage, thinly sliced and roughly chopped into 2-inch long pieces
1 can (15 ounces) black beans, rinsed and drained
1 red bell pepper, chopped
⅓ cup chopped green onions, both green and white parts
⅓ cup chopped fresh cilantro

2 to 3 tablespoons fresh lime juice, to taste
1 teaspoon olive oil
¼ teaspoon salt
Avocado salsa verde
¾ cup mild salsa verde, either homemade or store-bought
1 ripe avocado, diced
⅓ cup fresh cilantro (a few stems are ok)
1 tablespoon fresh lime juice
1 medium garlic clove, roughly chopped
Optional garnishes: chopped fresh cilantro, crumbled feta and/or seasoned toasted pepitas

- To roast the spaghetti squash: Preheat the oven to 400 degrees Fahrenheit and line a large baking sheet with parchment paper for easy clean-up. On the baking sheet, drizzle the halved spaghetti squash with olive oil. Rub the olive oil all over each of the halves, adding more if necessary.

- Sprinkle the insides of the squash with freshly ground black pepper and salt. Turn them over so the insides are facing down. Roast for 40 to 60 minutes, until the flesh is easily pierced through with a fork.

- Meanwhile, to assemble the slaw: In a medium mixing bowl, combine the cabbage, black beans, bell pepper, green onion, cilantro, lime juice, olive oil and salt. Toss to combine and set aside to marinate.

- To make the salsa verde: In the bowl of a blender or food processor, combine the avocado, salsa verde, cilantro, lime juice and garlic. Blend until smooth, pausing to scrape down the sides as necessary.

- To assemble, first use a fork to separate and fluff up the flesh of the spaghetti squash. Then divide the slaw into each of the spaghetti squash "bowls," and add a big dollop of avocado salsa verde. Finish the bowls with another sprinkle of pepper, cilantro and optional crumbled feta or pepitas.

Per Serving: Calories: 362; Total Fat: 1g; Saturated Fat: 0g; Protein: 17g; Carbs: 60g; Fiber: 20g; Sugar: 4g

Spicy Sweet Potato and Green Rice Burrito Bowls

Serves: 4 / Preparation time: 20 minutes / Cooking time: 45 minutes

Green rice
3 tablespoons extra-virgin olive oil
1 ½ cups long grain brown rice
3 cups vegetable broth
1 ½ cup baby spinach, lightly packed
½ cup cilantro (mostly leaves, stems are ok), lightly packed
1 jalapeño or serrano pepper, seeded, membranes removed and roughly chopped
1 medium shallot, peeled and roughly chopped
1 garlic clove, peeled, roughly chopped
¼ teaspoon salt, more to taste
Sweet potatoes
2 pounds sweet potatoes (3 to 4 medium sweet potatoes), peeled and sliced into 1-inch chunks
2 tablespoons olive oil

½ teaspoon smoked paprika
¼ teaspoon sea salt
Seasoned black beans
2 cans (14 ounces each) black beans or 3 cups cooked black beans, with their cooking liquid
2 teaspoons ground cumin
½ teaspoon chili powder
1 teaspoon sherry vinegar or lime juice
Sea salt and freshly ground black pepper, to taste
Additional garnishes
¼ cup pepitas (green pumpkin seeds)
¼ teaspoon olive oil
1 avocado, pitted and sliced
Jarred mild salsa verde
Chopped cilantro

- To roast the spaghetti squash: Preheat the oven to 400 degrees Fahrenheit and line a large baking sheet with parchment paper for easy clean-up. On the baking sheet, drizzle the halved spaghetti squash with olive oil. Rub the olive oil all over each of the halves, adding more if necessary.
- Sprinkle the insides of the squash with freshly ground black pepper and salt. Turn them over so the insides are facing down. Roast for 40 to 60 minutes, until the flesh is easily pierced through with a fork.
- Meanwhile, to assemble the slaw: In a medium mixing bowl, combine the cabbage, black beans, bell pepper, green onion, cilantro, lime juice, olive oil and salt. Toss to combine and set aside to marinate.
- To make the salsa verde: In the bowl of a blender or food processor, combine the avocado, salsa verde, cilantro, lime juice and garlic. Blend until smooth, pausing to scrape down the sides as necessary.
- To assemble, first use a fork to separate and fluff up the flesh of the spaghetti squash. Then divide the slaw into each of the spaghetti squash "bowls," and add a big dollop of avocado salsa verde. Finish the bowls with another sprinkle of pepper, cilantro and optional crumbled feta or pepitas.

Per Serving: Calories: 784; Total Fat: 27g; Saturated Fat: 4g; Protein: 20g; Carbs: 118g; Fiber: 24g; Sugar: 8g

Pinto Posole

Serves: 4 / Preparation time: 20 minutes / Cooking time: 30 minutes

2 to 4 guajillo chili peppers
2 tablespoons extra-virgin olive oil
1 large white onion, finely chopped
4 cloves garlic, pressed or minced
1 tablespoon ground cumin
½ cup (4 ounces) tomato paste
1 bay leaf
3 cans (15 ounces each) pinto beans, rinsed and drained

1 can (15 ounces) hominy, rinsed and drained
32 ounces (4 cups) vegetable broth
2 cups water
½ teaspoon fine sea salt, to taste
¼ cup chopped cilantro, divided
1 lime, halved
Recommended garnishes: sliced avocado, shredded green cabbage, chopped radish, onion and/or jalapeño

- Cut off the stem ends of the chilis and shake/flick the chilis to remove as many seeds as possible (it's ok if some remain). Rinse them and pat them dry.
- Heat an empty Dutch oven or soup pot over medium heat until a few drops of water evaporate quickly from the pan. Toast the chilis in the dry pan, pressing them flat with a spatula for a few seconds until fragrant, then flip them over and press them again for a few seconds. Remove the toasted chilis and set them aside for now.
- In the same pot (still over medium heat), warm the olive oil until shimmering. Add the onion and a pinch of salt. Cook, stirring often, until the onions are tender and translucent, about 5 minutes.
- Add the garlic and cumin and cook until fragrant while stirring, about 1 minute. Add the tomato paste and cook, while stirring, for 1 minute.
- Add the toasted chili peppers, bay leaf, hominy, beans, vegetable broth and water to the pot. Stir in ½ teaspoon salt and raise the heat to medium-high. Bring the mixture to a simmer, then reduce heat as necessary to maintain a gentle simmer, stirring occasionally, and cook for 25 minutes.
- Remove the chili peppers and bay leaf from the soup and discard them. Stir the cilantro and juice of ½ lime into the soup. Taste, and add more salt (I usually add at least ¼ teaspoon more) and/or lime juice if necessary. For extra richness, add a little splash of olive oil and stir it in.
- Cut the remaining lime into small wedges. Divide the soup into bowls and garnish with lime wedges and other garnishes of your choice.

Per Serving: Calories: 268; Total Fat: 5g; Saturated Fat: 1g; Protein: 12g; Carbs: 43g; Fiber: 12g; Sugar: 4g

Burrito-Stuffed Sweet Potatoes

Serves: 4 / Preparation time: 20 minutes / Cooking time: 45 minutes

4 small sweet potatoes (mine came to about 2 ½ pounds total)
½ cup uncooked brown basmati rice, rinsed
1 cup cooked black beans (I used canned, rinsed and drained)
1 teaspoon ground cumin
½ garlic clove, minced
½ teaspoon olive oil
1 teaspoon tomato paste
Pinch of salt
Rustic salsa
1 yellow or red bell pepper, seeded and chopped
1 cup cherry tomatoes, halved
½ small red onion, chopped (mine came to about ¾ cup chopped)

1 tablespoon fresh lime juice
2 tablespoon chopped fresh cilantro leaves
1 ½ teaspoons olive oil
Salt and pepper, to taste
Guacamole
1 ripe, medium avocado
½ clove garlic, minced
1 tablespoon fresh lime juice
2 tablespoons chopped fresh cilantro leaves
Generous pinch of salt
For serving
Shredded cabbage (Laura used green; I used purple) or romaine lettuce
Hot sauce (optional)

- Preheat the oven to 400 degrees Fahrenheit. Line a baking dish with parchment paper.
- Place the sweet potatoes in the baking dish, and prick each one a couple of times with a fork. Slide the sweet potatoes into the oven and bake until very tender, about 45 minutes (mine took 5 to 10 minutes extra since they were a little bigger than specified).
- In a medium saucepan, combine the basmati rice, black beans, cumin, garlic, olive oil, tomato paste and salt. Pour 1 ¼ cups water into the pot. Cover and bring to a boil over medium heat. Lower the heat to a simmer, and cook until all of the liquid is absorbed, about 40 minutes. Cover and set aside to keep the rice warm.
- Make the rustic salsa: In a medium bowl, combine the bell pepper, cherry tomatoes, red onions, lime juice, cilantro and olive oil. Season the mixture with salt and pepper, and toss to combine. Set aside.
- Make the guacamole: Peel the avocado and extract the pit. Place the avocado flesh in a medium bowl and mash with a fork. Once you've broken it up a bit, add the garlic, lime juice, cilantro and salt. Mash the avocado until the seasoning is evenly distributed and you have a chunky paste. Set aside.
- Place each baked sweet potato in a shallow bowl. Cut along the top of the sweet potato and pull back the skin. Spilt the sweet potatoes a little bit to make room for the fillings.
- Divide the rice and bean mixture among the sweet potatoes (spillover is fine!). Top each bowl with ¼th of the rustic salsa. Finish each plate with a dollop of the guacamole and some shredded cabbage on top. Serve with hot sauce on the side if you wish.

Per Serving: Calories: 414; Total Fat: 13g; Saturated Fat: 2g; Protein: 9g; Carbs: 68g; Fiber: 13g; Sugar: 14g

Butternut Squash Chipotle Chili with Avocado

Serves: 4 / Preparation time: 20 minutes / Cooking time: 60 minutes

2 tablespoons olive oil
1 medium red onion, chopped
2 red bell peppers, chopped
1 small butternut squash (1 ½ pounds or less), peeled and chopped into ½-inch cubes
4 garlic cloves, pressed or minced
1 tablespoon chili powder
½+ tablespoon chopped chipotle pepper in adobo (start with ½ tablespoon and add more to taste, I thought mine was just right with 1 tablespoon)
1 teaspoon ground cumin
¼ teaspoon ground cinnamon

1 bay leaf
2 cans (15 ounces each) black beans, rinsed and drained, or 3 cups cooked black beans
1 small can (14 ounces) diced tomatoes, including the liquid**
2 cups vegetable broth (or one 14-ounce can)
Salt, to taste
2 Avocados from Mexico, diced
3 corn tortillas for crispy tortilla strips (or substitute crumbled tortilla chips)
Optional additional garnishes: Chopped fresh cilantro and/or red pepper flakes

- In a 4- to 6-quart Dutch oven or stockpot over medium heat, warm the olive oil until shimmering. Add the onion, bell pepper and butternut squash and cook, stirring occasionally, until the onions are turning translucent.
- Turn the heat down to medium-low and add the garlic, chili powder, ½ tablespoon chopped chipotle peppers, cumin and cinnamon. Cook, stirring constantly, until fragrant, about 30 seconds. Add the bay leaf, black beans, tomatoes and their juices and broth. Stir to combine and cover for about 1 hour, stirring occasionally. Taste about halfway through cooking and add more chopped chipotle peppers if you'd like.
- You'll know your chili is done when the butternut squash is nice and tender and the liquid has reduced a bit, producing the hearty chili consistency we all know and love. Remove the bay leaf and add salt to taste.
- To make the crispy tortilla strips: stack the corn tortillas and slice them into thin little strips, about 2 inches long by ¼ inch wide. Warm a drizzle of olive oil in a medium pan over medium heat until shimmering. Toss in the tortilla slices, sprinkle with salt and stir. Cook until the strips are crispy and turning golden, stirring occasionally, about 4 to 7 minutes. Remove tortilla strips from skillet and drain on a plate covered with a piece of paper towel.
- Serve the chili in individual bowls, topped with crispy tortilla strips and plenty of diced avocado. I added a little sprinkle of red pepper flakes (optional). Cilantro would be nice as well. You might want to serve this along with some chipotle hot sauce (Tobasco makes one) for the spice addicts like myself.

Per Serving: Calories: 591; Total Fat: 23g; Saturated Fat: 3g; Protein: 20g; Carbs: 84g; Fiber: 23g; Sugar: 12g

Kale Salad with Green Tahini Dressing

Serves: 4 / Preparation time: 15 minutes / Cooking time: 0 minutes

Per salad
½ medium bunch kale, preferably the Tuscan/lacinato variety, or several handfuls of your favorite greens
1 cup leftover cooked grains (I love long-grain brown rice, quinoa, farro or wheat berries…)
2 carrots, sliced into long ribbons with a julienne peeler or regular veggie peeler
1 radish, thinly sliced and roughly chopped
2 tablespoons pepitas (green pumpkin seeds) or sunflower seeds, toasted
More ideas: halved cherry tomatoes, sliced avocado, chopped bell pepper, whatever else strikes your fancy…

Green tahini dressing (yields about ¾ cup, so you'll have plenty for future salads)
⅓ cup olive oil
⅓ cup lime juice (about 3 to 4 medium limes)
Handful of fresh cilantro
1 small jalapeño, seeds and membranes removed, roughly chopped
2 tablespoons tahini
1 ½ teaspoons honey or maple syrup
½ teaspoon ground cumin
1 clove garlic, roughly chopped
¼ teaspoon fine-grain sea salt, to taste
Pinch of red pepper flakes, optional for extra heat

- To prepare the kale (skip this step if you're using any other kind of fresh green), first use a sharp chef's knife to remove the center ribs from the kale, then discard the ribs. Chop the kale into small, bite-sized pieces. Then, sprinkle the kale lightly with salt, and massage the kale by scrunching handfuls at a time until the kale is darker in color and fragrant. This step reduces the bitterness in the kale and improves its texture.
- In a bowl, combine the prepared kale, leftover grains (I like to warm mine a bit in the microwave first), carrot, radishes, toasted pepitas, and/or your toppings of choice.
- To make the dressing: Combine all of the ingredients in a blender or food processor and blend until smooth, pausing to scrape down the sides as necessary. Taste, and blend in additional salt if the dressing needs a little more oomph. If you'd like spicier dressing, blend in a pinch of red pepper flakes. If the dressing is too bold for your liking, dilute it with a little more olive oil and blend again.
- Drizzle the green tahini dressing generously over the salad (you'll still have plenty leftover) and enjoy.

Per Serving: Calories: 397; Total Fat: 19g; Saturated Fat: 3g; Protein: 11g; Carbs: 49g; Fiber: 19g; Sugar: 8g

Thai Peanut & Quinoa Salad

Serves: 4 / Preparation time: 15 minutes / Cooking time: 50 minutes

Salad
¾ cup uncooked quinoa or millet
1 ½ cups water
2 cups shredded purple cabbage
1 cup grated carrot
1 cup thinly sliced snow peas or sugar snap peas
½ cup chopped cilantro
¼ cup thinly sliced green onion
¼ cup chopped roasted and salted peanuts, for garnish

Peanut sauce
¼ cup smooth peanut butter
3 tablespoons reduced-sodium tamari or soy sauce
1 tablespoon maple syrup or honey
1 tablespoon rice vinegar
1 teaspoon toasted sesame oil
1 teaspoon grated fresh ginger (I love ginger so I used 2 teaspoons)
½ lime, juiced (about 1 ½ tablespoons)
Pinch of red pepper flakes

- Cook the quinoa: First, rinse the quinoa in a fine mesh colander under running water. In a medium-sized pot, combine the rinsed quinoa and 1 ½ cups water. Bring the mixture to a gentle boil over medium heat, then reduce the heat to medium-low and gently simmer the quinoa until it has absorbed all of the water. Remove the quinoa from heat, cover the pot and let it rest for 5 minutes. Uncover the pot and fluff the quinoa with a fork. Set it aside to cool.
- Meanwhile, make the peanut sauce: Whisk together the peanut butter and tamari until smooth (if this is difficult, microwave the mixture for up to 30 seconds to loosen it up). Add the remaining ingredients and whisk until smooth. If the mixture seems too thick to toss into the salad, whisk in a bit of water to loosen it up (I didn't need to do this).
- In a large serving bowl, combine the cooked quinoa, shredded cabbage, carrot, snow peas, cilantro and green onion. Toss to combine, then pour in the peanut sauce. Toss again until everything it lightly coated in sauce. Taste, and if it doesn't taste quite amazing yet, add a pinch of salt and toss again. Divide into individual bowls and garnish with peanuts.
- This salad keeps well, covered and refrigerated, for about 4 days. If you don't want your chopped peanuts to get soggy, store them separately from the rest and garnish just before serving.

Per Serving: Calories: 260; Total Fat: 13g; Saturated Fat: 0g; Protein: 8g; Carbs: 27g; Fiber: 4g; Sugar: 7g

Crispy Falafel

Serves: 4 / Preparation time: 15 minutes / Cooking time: 30 minutes

¼ cup + 1 tablespoon extra-virgin olive oil

1 cup dried (uncooked/raw) chickpeas, rinsed, picked over and soaked for at least 4 hours and up to 24 hours in the refrigerator

½ cup roughly chopped red onion (about ½ small red onion)

½ cup packed fresh parsley (mostly leaves but small stems are ok)

½ cup packed fresh cilantro (mostly leaves but small stems are ok)

4 cloves garlic, quartered

1 teaspoon fine sea salt

½ teaspoon (about 25 twists) freshly ground black pepper

½ teaspoon ground cumin

¼ teaspoon ground cinnamon

- With an oven rack in the middle position, preheat oven to 375 degrees Fahrenheit. Pour ¼ cup of the olive oil into a large, rimmed baking sheet and turn until the pan is evenly coated.
- In a food processor, combine the soaked and drained chickpeas, onion, parsley, cilantro, garlic, salt, pepper, cumin, cinnamon, and the remaining 1 tablespoon of olive oil. Process until smooth, about 1 minute.
- Using your hands, scoop out about 2 tablespoons of the mixture at a time. Shape the falafel into small patties, about 2 inches wide and ½ inch thick. Place each falafel on your oiled pan.
- Bake for 25 to 30 minutes, carefully flipping the falafels halfway through baking, until the falafels are deeply golden on both sides. These falafels keep well in the refrigerator for up to 4 days, or in the freezer for several months.

Per Serving: Calories: 100; Total Fat: 5g; Saturated Fat: 1g; Protein: 4g; Carbs: 15g; Fiber: 4g; Sugar: 1g

Thai Red Curry with Vegetables

Serves: 4 / Preparation time: 15 minutes / Cooking time: 30 minutes

1 ¼ cups brown jasmine rice or long-grain brown rice, rinsed

1 tablespoon coconut oil or olive oil

1 small white onion, chopped (about 1 cup)

Pinch of salt, more to taste

1 tablespoon finely grated fresh ginger (about a 1-inch nub of ginger)

2 cloves garlic, pressed or minced

1 red bell pepper, sliced into thin 2-inch long strips

1 yellow, orange or green bell pepper, sliced into thin 2-inch long strips

3 carrots, peeled and sliced on the diagonal into ¼-inch thick rounds (about 1 cup)

2 tablespoons Thai red curry paste

1 can (14 ounces) regular coconut milk

½ cup water

1 ½ cups packed thinly sliced kale (tough ribs removed first), preferably the Tuscan/lacinato/dinosaur variety

1 ½ teaspoons coconut sugar or turbinado (raw) sugar or brown sugar

1 tablespoon tamari or soy sauce

2 teaspoons rice vinegar or fresh lime juice

Garnishes/sides: handful of chopped fresh basil or cilantro, optional red pepper flakes, optional sriracha or chili garlic sauce

- To cook the rice, bring a large pot of water to boil. Add the rinsed rice and continue boiling for 30 minutes, reducing heat as necessary to prevent overflow. Remove from heat, drain the rice and return the rice to pot. Cover and let the rice rest for 10 minutes or longer, until you're ready to serve. Just before serving, season the rice to taste with salt and fluff it with a fork.

- To make the curry, warm a large skillet with deep sides over medium heat. Once it's hot, add the oil. Add the onion and a sprinkle of salt and cook, stirring often, until the onion has softened and is turning translucent, about 5 minutes. Add the ginger and garlic and cook until fragrant, about 30 seconds, while stirring continuously.

- Add the bell peppers and carrots. Cook until the bell peppers are fork-tender, 3 to 5 more minutes, stirring occasionally. Then add the curry paste and cook, stirring often, for 2 minutes.

- Add the coconut milk, water, kale and sugar, and stir to combine. Bring the mixture to a simmer over medium heat. Reduce heat as necessary to maintain a gentle simmer and cook until the peppers, carrots and kale have softened to your liking, about 5 to 10 minutes, stirring occasionally.

- Remove the pot from the heat and season with tamari and rice vinegar. Add salt (I added ¼ teaspoon for optimal flavor), to taste. If the curry needs a little more punch, add ½ teaspoon more tamari, or for more acidity, add ½ teaspoon more rice vinegar. Divide rice and curry into bowls and garnish with chopped cilantro and a sprinkle of red pepper flakes, if you'd like. If you love spicy curries, serve with sriracha or chili garlic sauce on the side.

Per Serving: Calories: 340; Total Fat: 11g; Saturated Fat: 8g; Protein: 8g; Carbs: 56g; Fiber: 6g; Sugar: 9g

Roasted Butternut Squash Tacos

Serves: 4 / Preparation time: 15 minutes / Cooking time: 30 minutes

Roasted butternut squash

1 medium butternut squash (about 2 to 2 ½ pounds, I used two 12-ounce bags of pre-sliced butternut from Trader Joe's), peeled and sliced into ¾-inch cubes

2 tablespoons olive oil

1 teaspoon chili powder

Salt and freshly ground pepper

Cabbage and black bean slaw

2 cups purple cabbage, thinly sliced and roughly chopped into 2-inch long pieces

2 cans black beans (15 ounces each), rinsed and drained, or 3 cups cooked black beans

⅓ cup chopped green onions, both green and white parts

⅓ cup chopped fresh cilantro

2 to 3 tablespoons fresh lime juice, to taste

1 teaspoon olive oil

¼ teaspoon salt, more to taste

Simple guacamole (double if you love guac!)

1 large avocado, diced

1 tablespoon lime juice

¼ teaspoon ground coriander (optional)

Pinch of salt, more to taste

Everything else

8 corn tortillas (certified gluten free if necessary)

Optional garnishes: additional chopped cilantro, hot sauce, toasted pepitas, crumbled feta cheese (omit for vegan tacos)

- Preheat oven to 425 degrees Fahrenheit. Line one large, rimmed baking sheet with parchment paper for easier cleanup.

- To roast the squash: On your prepared baking sheet, toss the cubed butternut in enough olive oil to lightly coat all sides, about 2 tablespoons. Sprinkle with 1 teaspoon chili pepper and a pinch of salt and pepper. Arrange the butternut in a single layer. Bake until the butternut is tender throughout and caramelized on the edges, about 30 to 35 minutes, tossing halfway.

- Meanwhile, to assemble the slaw: In a medium mixing bowl, combine the cabbage, black beans, green onion, cilantro, lime juice, olive oil and salt. Toss to combine, then taste and add additional lime juice and/or salt if necessary. Set aside to marinate.

- To prepare the guacamole: In a small bowl, combine the diced avocado, lime juice, coriander and salt. Mash with a pastry cutter, potato masher or fork until the mixture is blended and no longer chunky. Taste and add additional salt if necessary.

- To warm the tortillas: In a small skillet over medium heat, warm each tortilla on both sides before transferring to a plate and covering with a lint-free towel to keep warm. Repeat with each tortilla, stacking each warmed tortilla on the last.

- To assemble the tacos, spoon an ample amount of slaw down the center of your taco, top with roasted butternut and spread a spoonful of guacamole down the side. Top with garnishes of your choice and serve immediately.

Per Serving: Calories: 274; Total Fat: 5g; Saturated Fat: 2g; Protein: 12g; Carbs: 56g; Fiber: 13g; Sugar: 4g

Peanut Slaw with Soba Noodles

Serves: 4 / Preparation time: 20 minutes / Cooking time: 5 minutes

Slaw
4 ounces soba noodles or whole wheat spaghetti
1 very small purple or green cabbage, sliced into quarters and core removed (about 16 ounces/6 cups shredded)
½ pound (about 12) Brussels sprouts, nubby ends removed, or additional cabbage (about 2 cups shredded)
4 carrots, peeled
1 bunch of green onions, trimmed and sliced into thin rounds
Peanut-sesame dressing
½ cup peanut butter

3 tablespoons white wine vinegar or rice vinegar
3 tablespoons toasted sesame oil
3 tablespoons reduced-sodium tamari or other soy sauce
2 tablespoons honey or maple syrup
1 tablespoon finely grated fresh ginger
2 garlic cloves, pressed or minced
Garnish
Sprinkle of coarsely chopped peanuts
Handful of cilantro, coarsely torn
1 lime, sliced into wedges
Optional, for spice lovers: sriracha or chili-garlic sauce

- Cook the soba noodles: Bring a large pot of water to boil and cook the noodles according to package directions. Drain and rinse with cold water before returning to pot.
- Prepare the vegetables: This is easier in a food processor than by hand. If using a food processor, shred the cabbage and sprouts with the slicing disk, then grate the carrots using the grating disk. Or use a chef's knife to chop the cabbage and sprouts into thin strips, then coarsely grate the carrots.
- Prepare the dressing: In a 2-cup liquid measuring cup or medium bowl, whisk together the dressing ingredients until smooth. If the mixture should be thick but drizzly; if it's too thick, whisk in water in 1 tablespoon increments until it is (at which point you might need to add a little salt, to taste, since the flavors have been diluted.)
- In a large serving bowl, combine the cooked soba noodles, shredded cabbage and sprouts, grated carrots, and chopped green onions. Pour dressing over the vegetables and toss to coat (you may or may not need all of the dressing). For best flavor, let the slaw marinate for 20 minutes before serving.
- Serve slaw with a sprinkling of chopped peanuts, torn cilantro and a lime wedge. Serve with sriracha on the side, if you'd like a spicy kick. This slaw keeps very well for a few days (covered and refrigerated). Before serving, wake up the flavors with a dash of lime juice or vinegar and more fresh cilantro.

Per Serving: Calories: 152; Total Fat: 9g; Saturated Fat: 1g; Protein: 6g; Carbs: 17g; Fiber: 3g; Sugar: 4g

Buddha Bowl

Serves: 4 / Preparation time: 30 minutes / Cooking time: 30 minutes

Rice and veggies
1 ¼ cups short-grain brown rice or long-grain brown rice, rinsed
1 ½ cups frozen shelled edamame, preferably organic
1 ½ cups trimmed and roughly chopped snap peas or snow peas, or thinly sliced broccoli florets
1 to 2 tablespoons reduced-sodium tamari or soy sauce, to taste
4 cups chopped red cabbage or spinach or romaine lettuce or kale (ribs removed)

2 ripe avocados, halved, pitted and thinly sliced into long strips (wait to slice just before serving, see details in step 5)
Essential garnishes
1 small cucumber, very thinly sliced
Carrot ginger dressing
Thinly sliced green onion (about ½ small bunch)
Lime wedges
Toasted sesame oil, for drizzling
Sesame seeds
Flaky sea salt

- Bring a large pot of water to boil (ideally about 4 quarts water). Once the water is boiling, add the rice and continue boiling for 25 minutes. Add the edamame and cook for 3 more minutes (it's ok if the water doesn't reach a rapid boil again). Then add the snap peas and cook for 2 more minutes.

- Drain well, and return the rice and veggies to the pot. Season to taste with 1 to 2 tablespoons of tamari or soy sauce, and stir to combine.

- Divide the rice/veggie mixture and raw veggies into 4 bowls. Arrange cucumber slices along the edge of the bowl (see photos). Drizzle lightly with carrot ginger dressing and top with sliced green onion. Place a lime wedge or 2 in each bowl.

- When you're ready to serve, divide the avocado into the bowls. Lightly drizzle sesame oil over the avocado, followed by a generous sprinkle of sesame seeds and flaky sea salt. Serve promptly.

- If you intend to have leftovers, wait to complete step 4 just before serving (otherwise the avocado will brown too soon). Leftover bowls keep well (avocado excluded) for 4 to 5 days in the refrigerator.

Per Serving: Calories: 683; Total Fat: 31g; Saturated Fat: 5g; Protein: 34g; Carbs: 68g; Fiber: 9g; Sugar: 9g

Thai Green Curry with Spring Vegetables

Serves: 4 / Preparation time: 15 minutes / Cooking time: 30 minutes

1 cup brown basmati rice, rinsed
2 teaspoons coconut oil or olive oil
1 small white onion, diced
1 tablespoon finely chopped fresh ginger
(about a 1-inch nub of ginger, peeled and
chopped)
2 cloves garlic, finely chopped
Pinch of salt
½ bunch asparagus, tough ends removed
and sliced into 2-inch long pieces (to yield
about 2 cups prepared asparagus)
3 carrots, peeled and sliced on the diagonal
into ¼-inch wide rounds (to yield about 1
cup sliced carrots)

2 tablespoons Thai green curry paste
1 can (14 ounces) coconut milk (I used full-
fat coconut milk for a richer curry)
½ cup water
1 ½ teaspoons coconut sugar or turbinado
(raw) sugar or brown sugar
2 cups packed baby spinach, roughly
chopped
1 ½ teaspoons rice vinegar or fresh lime
juice
1 ½ teaspoons soy sauce (I used reduced-
sodium tamari)
Garnishes: handful of chopped fresh
cilantro and red pepper flakes, to taste

- To cook the rice, bring a large pot of water to boil. Add the rinsed rice and continue boiling for 30 minutes, reducing heat as necessary to prevent overflow. Remove from heat, drain the rice and return the rice to pot. Cover and let the rice rest for 10 minutes or longer, until you're ready to serve.

- Warm a large skillet with deep sides over medium heat. Once it's hot, add a couple teaspoons of oil. Cook the onion, ginger and garlic with a sprinkle of salt for about 5 minutes, stirring often. Add the asparagus and carrots and cook for 3 more minutes, stirring occasionally. Then add the curry paste and cook, stirring often, for 2 minutes.

- Pour the coconut milk into the pan, along with ½ cup water and 1 ½ teaspoons sugar. Bring the mixture to a simmer. Reduce heat as necessary to maintain a gentle simmer and cook until the carrots and asparagus are tender and cooked through, about 5 to 10 minutes.

- Once the vegetables are done cooking, stir the spinach into the mixture and cook until the spinach has wilted, about 30 seconds. Remove the curry from heat and season with rice vinegar and soy sauce. Add salt and red pepper flakes (optional), to taste. Divide rice and curry into bowls and garnish with chopped cilantro and a sprinkle of red pepper flakes, if you'd like.

Per Serving: Calories: 152; Total Fat: 9g; Saturated Fat: 1g; Protein: 6g; Carbs: 17g; Fiber: 3g; Sugar: 4g

Thai Mango Cabbage Wraps with Crispy Tofu and Peanut Sauce

Serves: 4 / Preparation time: 30 minutes / Cooking time: 30 minutes

Crispy baked tofu
1 (15 ounce) block of organic extra-firm tofu
1 tablespoon olive oil
1 tablespoon reduced-sodium tamari or soy sauce
2 teaspoons arrowroot starch or cornstarch
Peanut sauce
⅓ cup creamy peanut butter
2 tablespoons white wine vinegar or apple cider vinegar
2 tablespoons reduced-sodium tamari or soy sauce
2 tablespoons honey or agave nectar or maple syrup
2 teaspoons toasted sesame oil
½ lime, juiced

2 garlic cloves, pressed or minced
Mango pico
2 ripe mangos, diced
1 medium red bell pepper, chopped
½ bunch (about 4) green onions, chopped
⅓ cup packed fresh cilantro leaves, chopped
1 jalapeño, minced
½ lime, juiced
⅛ teaspoon salt
Everything else
1 small head of green cabbage (the smaller, the better) or bibb lettuce
2 tablespoons large, unsweetened coconut flakes (optional)
2 tablespoons chopped peanuts (optional)

- To prepare the tofu: Preheat oven to 400 degrees Fahrenheit and line a rimmed baking sheet with parchment paper. Drain the tofu and use your palms to gently squeeze out some of the water. Slice the tofu into thirds so you have three ½-inch slabs. Transfer the tofu to a plate lined with a lint-free tea towel or paper towels. Fold the towel over one tofu slab, then place the other slab on top, then repeat with the last slab. Top with more towel and place something heavy on top (like a cast iron skillet) to help press the water out of the tofu.

- While the tofu drains, make the peanut sauce: Simply whisk together all of the sauce ingredients until well blended. If the flavor seems too bold or the sauce is too thick, thin it with a tablespoon or two of water. Set aside.

- To bake the tofu: Transfer the drained tofu to a cutting board. Slice each slab into four columns and four rows. Whisk together 1 tablespoon olive oil and tamari, then drizzle it over the tofu and toss to coat. Sprinkle 1 teaspoon arrowroot starch over the tofu, then toss the tofu until the starch is evenly incorporated. Repeat with 1 more teaspoon arrowroot starch. Arrange the tofu in an even layer on the baking sheet. Bake for 30 to 35 minutes, tossing halfway, until the tofu is crisp and deeply golden.

- To make the mango salsa: Combine ingredients in a small serving bowl and toss. Taste, and add additional salt and/or a little splash of white wine vinegar if necessary. Set aside.

- To prepare the cabbage/lettuce: Slice off the thick stem and bottom ¼th of the head of cabbage/lettuce. Gently pull off one leaf at a time. Repeat until you have 6 to 8 cabbage leaves.
- If you want to go the extra mile with the tofu: Once the tofu has finished baking, toast the coconut flakes and chopped peanuts in a medium skillet over medium heat, stirring frequently, until the coconut is golden on the edges. Add the tofu to the pan. Pour in ⅔rds of the peanut sauce and toss to coat. Cook, stirring frequently, until the tofu has absorbed the sauce and has turned golden on the edges. Transfer to a plate to cool.
- To assemble the cabbage wraps: Divide the salsa amongst the salad wraps. Top with tofu and additional peanut sauce. Serve!

Per Serving: Calories: 340; Total Fat: 20g; Saturated Fat: 3g; Protein: 21g; Carbs: 25g; Fiber: 8g; Sugar: 11g

Homemade Vegetarian Chili

Serves: 4 / Preparation time: 20 minutes / Cooking time: 40 minutes

2 tablespoons extra-virgin olive oil
1 medium red onion, chopped
1 large red bell pepper, chopped
2 medium carrots, chopped
2 ribs celery, chopped
½ teaspoon salt, divided
4 cloves garlic, pressed or minced
2 tablespoons chili powder
2 teaspoons ground cumin
1 ½ teaspoons smoked paprika
1 teaspoon dried oregano
1 large can (28 ounces) or 2 small cans (15 ounces each) diced tomatoes, with their juices

2 cans (15 ounces each) black beans, rinsed and drained
1 can (15 ounces) pinto beans, rinsed and drained
2 cups vegetable broth or water
1 bay leaf
2 tablespoons chopped fresh cilantro, plus more for garnishing
1 to 2 teaspoons sherry vinegar or red wine vinegar or lime juice, to taste
Garnishes: chopped cilantro, sliced avocado, tortilla chips

- In a large Dutch oven or heavy-bottomed pot over medium heat, warm the olive oil until shimmering. Add the chopped onion, bell pepper, carrot, celery and ¼ teaspoon of the salt. Stir to combine and cook, stirring occasionally, until the vegetables are tender and the onion is translucent, about 7 to 10 minutes.
- Add the garlic, chili powder, cumin, smoked paprika and oregano. Cook until fragrant while stirring constantly, about 1 minute.
- Add the diced tomatoes and their juices, the drained black beans and pinto beans, vegetable broth and bay leaf. Stir to combine and let the mixture come to a simmer. Continue cooking, stirring occasionally and reducing heat as necessary to maintain a gentle simmer, for 30 minutes. Remove the chili from the heat.
- For the best texture and flavor, transfer 1 ½ cups of the chili to a blender, making sure to get some of the liquid portion. Securely fasten the lid and blend until smooth (watch out for hot steam), then pour the blended mixture back into the pot. (Or, you can blend the chili briefly with an immersion blender, or mash the chili with a potato masher until it reaches a thicker, more chili-like consistency.)
- Add the chopped cilantro, stir to blend, and then mix in the vinegar, to taste. Add salt to taste, too—I added ¼ teaspoon more at this point. Divide the mixture into individual bowls and serve with garnishes of your choice. This chili will keep well in the refrigerator for about 4 days or you can freeze it for longer-term storage

Per Serving: Calories: 219; Total Fat: 2g; Saturated Fat: 0g; Protein: 15g; Carbs: 27g; Fiber: 2g; Sugar: 10g

Spicy Vegan Oaxacan Bowl

Serves: 4 / Preparation time: 15 minutes / Cooking time: 25 minutes

Spice Rub
2 teaspoons cumin
1 teaspoon ground chipotle (or swap out a mix of smoked paprika and chili powder)
½ teaspoon kosher salt
Sheet Pan ingredients
½ a red onion, cut in ½ inch wedges
1 medium yam or sweet potato- diced into ¾ inch cubes (leave skin on)
8 baby bell peppers, cut in half (or 1 regular red or yellow bell pepper, cut into strips)
½ cup pecans
2 teaspoons maple syrup

1 15-16 ounce can Seasoned Black Beans (Cuban style or Mexican style) or use regular black beans (see notes)
Garnish: Avocado, cilantro, scallions, Cabbage Slaw, Mexican Secret Sauce or Vegan Avocado Sauce
Quick Cabbage Slaw
¼ of a a red cabbage, shredded
1 tablespoon olive oil
¼ cup chopped cilantro or scallions or both
1 teaspoon coriander
1/8 teaspoon kosher salt
1 tablespoon lime juice

- Preheat oven to 425F
- Mix cumin, chipotle and salt together in a small bowl.
- Place onion, sweet potato and peppers on a parchment lined sheet pan. Drizzle onion and potato with a little olive oil and sprinkle generously with spice mix, tossing to coat all sides well. Use about ½ or ⅔ of the spice.
- Place in the oven for 20-30 minutes, tossing halfway through.
- On another smaller parchment-lined pan, toss the pecans with 2 teaspoons maple syrup and 1 teaspoon of the spice mix. Place in the oven for 10-12 minutes, until lightly browned. When you pull it out, give nuts a quick toss to loosen them up and "fluffen" them, so when they cool, they are easy to remove.
- Heat the seasoned beans in a small pot on the stove (see notes) and make the slaw. Finely chop or shred the cabbage and place in a medium bowl with the rest of the ingredients, toss. Taste, adjust lime and salt.
- Slice the avocado.
- When the veggies are fork tender, assemble the bowls. Divide the beans among 2-3 bowls. Divide all the veggies, placing them over the beans, and top with slaw and add the avocado.
- Serve with the Mexican Secret Sauce or Vegan Avocado sauce if you like, or sour cream and hot sauce— it's fine without though too.

Per Serving: Calories: 487; Total Fat: 18g; Saturated Fat: 8g; Protein: 16g; Carbs: 72g; Fiber: 18g; Sugar: 7g

Miso Sesame Cauliflower Rice Bowl with Tofu & Veggies

Serves: 4 / Preparation time: 15 minutes / Cooking time: 25 minutes

16 ounces riced cauliflower (about 4 cups)
2 medium zucchini, cubed (or one small sweet potato or butternut)
4 ounces mushrooms, quartered
¼ an onion, diced
8 ounces tofu or chicken, cubed
Drizzle olive oil, generous pinch salt, granulated garlic (or one clove minced)
Marinade
1 tablespoon miso

3 tablespoons hot water
2 tablespoons sesame oil
¼ teaspoon salt
1 teaspoon rice wine vinegar
1 teaspoon sesame seeds
Additional toppings : scallions, avocado, Braggs or Smoked Shoyu, Sriracha, Asian seaweed/sesame spice mix like Furikake or Gomasio, seeds (sesame, hemp, sunflower or pumpkin – for texture)

- Pre heat oven to 425F
- Make the marinade in a small bowl by whisking hot water with miso until smooth, then add the rest of the ingredients- sesame oil, vinegar, salt, sesame seeds.
- On an extra large, parchment-lined sheet pan (or two smaller pan) place the riced cauliflower, piled no higher than ½ inch, then the veggies in sections along with the tofu (and or chicken). Season the tofu (or chicken) with a little salt, then spoon the marinade over top, coating well, then spoon the remaining marinade over the veggies (not the cauliflower). Drizzle the cauliflower with a little olive oil and sprinkle with salt and pepper and granulated garlic (or toss in a finely minced clove of garlic).
- Place in the oven for 20 minutes, giving the veggies and cauliflower a quick toss, then bake 10- more minutes or until desired doneness.
- Divide among two bowls.
- Scatter with scallions, avocado, Asian spice, seeds, and drizzle with a little Braggs Liquid aminos (or smoked shoyu soy sauce is nice) and sriracha hot sauce.

Per Serving: Calories: 387; Total Fat: 28g; Saturated Fat: 5g; Protein: 19g; Carbs: 24g; Fiber: 5g; Sugar: 12g

Roasted Vegetable Salad

Serves: 4 / Preparation time: 15 minutes / Cooking time: 30 minutes

Roasted Fall Veggies
3 small parsnips, peeled
3 small carrots, peeled
½ a cauliflower
1 small yam
1 small delicata squash
olive oil
salt and pepper to taste
generous pinch cumin seed and fennel
seeds (optional)
Salad
1 bunch lacinato kale, stacked and thinly
sliced
8 ounces shredded brussel sprouts (or
slaw)
1 tablespoon olive oil

¼ teaspoon salt
1–2 cups cooked lentils (little black caviar
or french green)
optional additions – golden raisins, pumpkin
seeds (or maple glazed pecans),
pomegranate seeds
Indian Curry Dressing
1 small shallot, finely diced
2 tablespoons olive oil
3 tablespoons apple cider vinegar
2 tablespoons maple syrup
¼ teaspoon salt
¼ teaspoon pepper
1 teaspoons yellow curry powder, more to
taste

- Preheat oven to 425F
- Cut parsnips and carrots into quarters, vertically, then half again if necessary, to get them to ½ inch thick at widest part. Cut cauliflower into bit sized florets, and yam (no need to peel) into ½ inch thick half moons. Split squash in half, remove seeds (no need to peel) and cut into ½ inch thick slices. (Alternatively, you can cut them into rings, but will need to remove seeds from each ring.) Place all the veggies on two, parchment lined sheet pans and drizzle with olive oil, sprinkle with salt and pepper. Add a pinch of the fennel and cumin seeds to the cauliflower. Roast 30-35 minutes, tossing them halfway through.
- Place the shredded kale and brussel sprouts in a large bowl and massage with olive oil and salt for about 3-4 minutes. Add the lentils.
- Whisk the dressing ingredients together in a small bowl.
- When veggies are done let them cool to room temp. Add them to the kale-brussels sprout bowl and toss all with the curry dressing. Taste, adjust salt and pepper. If you want a stronger curry flavor, add more and toss it in.
- Top with seeds or nuts, golden raisins, and or pomegranate seeds.
- Serve at room temp, or store in the fridge until ready to serve. This salad keeps for several days.

Per Serving: Calories: 215; Total Fat: 7g; Saturated Fat: 2g; Protein: 7g; Carbs: 34g; Fiber: 9g; Sugar: 9g

Middle Eastern Salad Tacos

Serves: 4 / Preparation time: 15 minutes / Cooking time: 0 minutes

Middle Eastern Spiced Chickpeas

2 teaspoons olive oil

1 can chick peas, rinsed and drained

1 teaspoon sumac (optional – leave out or use za'atar)

1 teaspoon cumin

¼–½ teaspoon salt

1 teaspoon sesame seeds

½ cup Hummus – or Baba Ganoush (really delicious!) or Tahini Sauce (not tahini paste)

6 x 6 inch tortillas, warmed or lightly toasted

Salad

giant handful arugula (or other greens)

1 tomato, diced

2 turkish cucumbers, diced

1–2 tablespoon olive oil

1–2 tablespoon lemon juice

1 teaspoon ground coriander

¼ teaspoon salt, more to taste

Garnish 1-2 scallions, sliced, fresh herbs like cilantro, Italian parsley, mint or dill

- Heat oil in a medium skillet over medium heat. Add chickpeas and spices and salt. Warm through, stirring. During the last minute add the sesame seeds. Turn heat off.
- Toss the salad ingredients together in a medium bowl. Lightly toast the tortillas until warm and pliable.
- Assemble. Spread hummus or baba ganoush onto the warm tortilla. Top with warm chickpeas and a heaping mound of the salad. Sprinkle with herbs and scallions.

Per Serving: Calories: 418; Total Fat: 16g; Saturated Fat: 3g; Protein: 14g; Carbs: 57g; Fiber: 13g; Sugar: 8g

Eggplant Puttanesca with Roasted Spaghetti Squash

Serves: 4 / Preparation time: 15 minutes / Cooking time: 35 minutes

3 lb Spaghetti Squash- (or sub pasta noodles)
4 tablespoon olive oil- divided
1 medium eggplant – cut into a small dice (4 cups)
1 red onion- diced
4–6 cloves garlic- rough chopped
1 red bell pepper- diced
14 ounce can crushed or diced tomatoes
1 tablespoon dry Italian herbs (or sub oregano and thyme)

1 teaspoon kosher salt
¼ teaspoon red chili flakes, more to taste
Splash red wine
2 tablespoons capers, more to taste, plus a splash of the brine
3 tablespoons slice olives (like green or kalamata)
Garnish: fresh Italian parsley, grated Romano or Parmesan cheese, or a drizzle olive oil

- Pre heat oven to 425F
- Cut squash in half, scrape out seeds with a spoon and place open side down, on a parchment-lined baking sheet in the oven and roast for 30- 40 minutes or until tender. (You could this the night before and then refrigerate and reheat.)
- While the squash is roasting make the Eggplant Puttanesca sauce.
- In a large heavy bottom skillet or dutch oven, heat 3 tablespoons oil over med-high heat.
- Add diced onion and eggplant, and saute, stirring often for 4-5 minutes. Add garlic and red bell pepper, turn heat down to medium and continue cooking until eggplant is tender, about 10-12 more minutes, stirring occasionally.
- Add crushed tomatoes, a generous splash of wine, chili flakes, salt, pepper, Italian herbs, and simmer on low heat 5-10 more minutes. Add capers and olives.
- Taste, adjust salt, spice level and add more capers or olives to taste. Sometimes I'll add a little splash of the caper or olive brine, to bump up the flavor.
- When spaghetti squash is tender, scoop it out into a strainer, let it drain for a few minutes, then place a platter or bowl, and fluff and toss well with salt, pepper and 1 tablespoon olive oil.
- Divide among bowls and top with the eggplant puttanesca. Sprinkle with fresh Italian parsley and grated cheese (optional) or a drizzle olive oil. Alternatively you can serve this right out of the spaghetti squash shell (making sure to season the squash, mixing with a fork before topping with the putttanesca.

Per Serving: Calories: 227; Total Fat: 22g; Saturated Fat: 7g; Protein: 6g; Carbs: 57g; Fiber: 14g; Sugar: 26g

Sesame Cabbage Noodle Salad

Serves: 4 / Preparation time: 15 minutes / Cooking time: 20 minutes

2 ounces vermicelli rice noodles
½ head purple cabbage- finely sliced
4 scallions, sliced at a diagnol
⅛–¼ cup finely sliced red onion
12 ounces baked or seared tofu (see notes) or shredded chicken
1 bunch cilantro (chopped)
2– 3 tablespoon toasted sesame seeds
¼ cup roasted peanuts (optional)
handful sunflower sprouts (optional)
Sesame Dressing:

1 tablespoon olive oil
3 tablespoons toasted sesame oil
3 tablespoons rice wine vinegar
1 tablespoon honey (or agave or cane sugar)
1 teaspoon finely minced ginger (or ginger paste)
2 teaspoons soy sauce or GF Liquid Amino Acids
¾ teaspoon salt, more to taste
squeeze of lime

- Set water to boil for the noodles.
- Decide what tofu or chicken option you want to use and start that process. (see notes)
- Thinly slice the cabbage and add it to a big bowl. Add the scallions, red onion and cilantro and toss.
- Whisk the dressing ingredients together in a small bowl and toss with the cabbage.
- Soak the noodles in the hot water (turn heat off) for 1-2 minutes, stirring until just pliable. Do not boil the noodles! Just let them get tender and pliable. Al dente is perfect, they will get softer in the salad. Rinse with cold water, until they feel very cold. Drain well and add to the cabbage salad. Toss.
- Add your choice of protein. Sprinkle with sesame seeds and roasted peanuts and sprouts if using.
- Enjoy!

Per Serving: Calories: 250; Total Fat: 16g; Saturated Fat: 3g; Protein: 9g; Carbs: 19g; Fiber: 3g; Sugar: 6g

SOUPS AND STEWS

Contents

Simple vegan detox soup

Serves: 4 / Preparation time: 15 minutes / Cooking time: 5 minutes

1/2 pound pumpkin (225 g)

2 red onions

1/2 yellow bell pepper

1/4 head of broccoli (discard the stem)

2 celery sticks

10 cherry tomatoes

4 cups boiling water (1 l)

4 tbsp soy sauce or tamari

1 tsp ginger powder

1 tbsp garlic powder

1 tbsp onion powder

1 tbsp herbes de Provence

2 tbsp nutritional yeast

Lemon juice to taste

- Spiralize the pumpkin or chopped it finely with a knife. You can also use a peeler.
- Chop the rest of the veggies and place them with the pumpkin in a large pot. Add the water, soy sauce, spices (ginger, garlic and onion powder) and the herbs.
- Cook over medium-high heat for 5 to 10 minutes.
- When the soup is ready, add the nutritional yeast and the lemon juice just before serving, stir and enjoy!

Per Serving: Calories: 60; Total Fat: 1g; Saturated Fat: 0g; Protein: 3g; Carbs: 13g; Fiber: 5g; Sugar: 4g

Fat-free Spanish lentil stew

Serves: 4 / Preparation time: 10 minutes / Cooking time: 50 minutes

5 cups water (1 l + 250 ml)

1/2 onion

1 carrot

1/2 green bell pepper

1/2 red bell pepper

2 tbsp tomato paste

1/2 cup uncooked lentils (100 g)

1 pound potatoes (450 g)

2 tbsp dried oregano

1 tbsp sweet paprika

1 tsp sea salt

- Pour 2 cups of water (500 ml) into a large pot and bring it to a boil. Then add the veggies (chopped), except the potatoes and cook over medium-high heat for 10 minutes.
- Blend the sauce and pour it into the pot again.
- Add the tomato paste, stir and add the lentils and 3 cups of water more (750 ml). Cook over medium-high heat for 15 minutes.
- Add the potatoes (diced) and cook for another 20 minutes or until they're cooked.
- Add the oregano, paprika and salt, stir and cook for 5 minutes more.

Per Serving: Calories: 228; Total Fat: 10g; Saturated Fat: 2g; Protein: 9g; Carbs: 25g; Fiber: 10g; Sugar: 0g

Spanish pumpkin and chickpea stew

Serves: 4 / Preparation time: 10 minutes / Cooking time: 40 minutes

3 cups water (750 ml)	1 chopped medium potato
2 cloves of garlic	2 cups chopped raw pumpkin (230 g)
1/2 chopped onion	2 tsp sweet paprika
1/4 chopped green bell pepper	1/2 tsp ground ginger
1/4 red bell pepper	1 tbsp extra virgin olive oil
1/2 chopped tomato	15 oz cooked or canned chickpeas (425 g)
2 tbsp tomato paste	Fresh parsley for garnish

- Pour the water in a large pot and bring it to a boil. Then add the garlic, onion, red and bell pepper, tomato and tomato paste. Cook over medium-high heat for about 5 minutes.
- Place the soup in a blender and blend until smooth. Then pour it in the pot again.
- Add the potatoes and cook over medium-high heat for 10 minutes.
- Add the pumpkin and cook for 15 or 20 minutes more or until it's soft. The time may vary depending on the type of pumpkin you're using.
- Add the sweet paprika, the ginger and the oil and stir.
- Add the chickpeas and cook for another 5 minutes.
- Serve hot. I also added chopped fresh parsley for garnish (optional).

Per Serving: Calories: 110; Total Fat: 5g; Saturated Fat: 1g; Protein: 5g; Carbs: 11g; Fiber: 2g; Sugar: 1g

Mexican style tomato soup

Serves: 4 / Preparation time: 5 minutes / Cooking time: 15 minutes

2 tbsp extra virgin olive oil

½ red chili pepper

2 cloves of garlic

1 onion

A handful of fresh cilantro

1 10-ounce can Piquillo peppers or roasted red peppers (290 g)

2 14-ounce cans chopped tomatoes (800 g)

1 tsp ground cumin

½ cup coconut milk (125 ml)

Sea salt and black pepper to taste

Serve with lime, tortilla chips and chopped veggies (I added red chili pepper, cilantro, cherry tomatoes and red onion)

- Heat the oil in a large pot over medium-high heat. Add the red chili pepper, garlic and onion (chopped) and cook for two minutes.
- Add the rest of the ingredients and cook for about 10 or 15 minutes. Add some water or more coconut milk if you want.
- Blend the soup in a blender and serve with lime, tortilla chips and chopped veggies.

Per Serving: Calories: 126; Total Fat: 9g; Saturated Fat: 3g; Protein: 2g; Carbs: 10g; Fiber: 2g; Sugar: 1g

20-minute vegan Spanish fabada

Serves: 4 / Preparation time: 5 minutes / Cooking time: 15 minutes

2 tbsp extra virgin olive oil

4 cloves of garlic, sliced

1 onion, chopped

15 oz canned or cooked fabes, you can use cannellini beans instead(400 g)

1/2 or 1 cup water (depending the consistency you're looking for)

1 tbsp sweet paprika

1/2 tsp ground turmeric

2 bay leaves

1 tsp sea salt

Black pepper to taste

- Heat one tablespoon of oil in a large pot and cook the cloves of garlic and the onion over medium-high heat for about 2 or 3 minutes.
- Blend the veggies with 1/4 fabes or beans (50 g) and the water until smooth.
- Pour the mixture in the pot and add the rest of the ingredients, excluding the oil. Stir and cook over medium-high heat for 10 minutes.
- Remove from heat, add one tablespoon of extra virgin olive oil, stir and serve.

Per Serving: Calories: 332; Total Fat: 9g; Saturated Fat: 1g; Protein: 9g; Carbs: 50g; Fiber: 7g; Sugar: 4g

Sweet potato coconut curry soup

Serves: 4 / Preparation time: 10 minutes / Cooking time: 40 minutes

2 tbsp extra virgin olive oil

4 cloves of garlic

1/2 onion

1 14-ounce coconut milk can (400 ml)

2 cups vegetable broth

1 tbsp maple syrup

1/2 tsp ground ginger

2 tbsp curry powder

1/2 tsp ground turmeric

1 cup diced sweet potato (265 g)

Salt to taste

Toppings: tofu, red cabbage, broccoli and red bell pepper

- Heat the oil in a large pot over medium heat. Add the garlic and the onion (diced) and cook until golden brown.
- Add the rest of the ingredients and simmer until the sweet potatoes are soft.
- Transfer the soup to a blender and blend until smooth and creamy.
- Serve with your favorite toppings. I used raw veggies (red cabbage, broccoli and red bell pepper) and tofu (I cook it according to our vegan Caesar salad recipe, but you can also bake, sauté or fry the tofu).

Per Serving: Calories: 277; Total Fat: 16g; Saturated Fat: 9g; Protein: 3g; Carbs: 35g; Fiber: 3g; Sugar: 4g

15-minute cannellini bean stew

Serves: 4 / Preparation time: 15 minutes / Cooking time: 15 minutes

14 oz canned or cooked cannellini beans (400 g)

2 cups tomato sauce (500 g). Chopped tomatoes and tomato paste also work

1 1/2 cup dried tomatoes rehydrate with water or oil (80 g), chopped

1 cup corn kernels (135 g)

2 tbsp tahini

1 tbsp onion powder

1 tbsp garlic powder

1 tbsp sweet paprika

Black pepper to taste

- I rehydrate the sun dried tomatoes in a bowl with warm or hot water for at least 20 minutes or until they're soft. I keep them in an airtight container for a few days. Feel free to use store bought sun dried tomatoes in olive oil and drain the oil.
- Mix all the ingredients in a pan and cook for 10 or 15 minutes.
- Serve the stew with some lamb's lettuce and sesame seeds (optional).

Per Serving: Calories: 192; Total Fat: 3g; Saturated Fat: 0g; Protein: 10g; Carbs: 27g; Fiber: 5g; Sugar: 4g

Simple vegan Miso soup

Serves: 4 / Preparation time: 10 minutes / Cooking time: 5 minutes

1.5 oz noodles (40 g)	1 tbsp dried wakame seaweed
3 tbsp miso	3.5 oz soft tofu (100 g)
4 cups water (1 l)	½ cup onion (60 g)

- Cook noodles according to package directions. Drain and set aside.
- Heat the water in a pot and when it starts to boil, add the dried wakame seaweed and cook over medium heat for about 5 minutes.
- Add the miso paste into a small bowl, add some hot water and whisk until smooth. Add to the soup after removing the pot from the heat and stir.
- Add the tofu and the green onion and stir again. You can cook the tofu and the green onion if you want for 5 minutes, although it's not necessary. Don't cook the miso paste.

Per Serving: Calories: 77; Total Fat: 2g; Saturated Fat: 1g; Protein: 6g; Carbs: 8g; Fiber: 3g; Sugar: 3g

Super satisfying vegan quinoa chili

Serves: 4 / Preparation time: 20 minutes / Cooking time: 35 minutes

1 tablespoon extra virgin olive oil

2 cloves of garlic

½ onion

1 chili or cayenne pepper or a pinch of cayenne powder

2 tomatoes

1 cup tomato sauce (270 grams)

1 tablespoon dried cilantro

1 tablespoon cumin

1 tablespoon paprika

Black pepper to taste

1 cup cooked quinoa (185 grams)

1 cup corn kernels (150 grams)

1 cup cooked red beans (115 grams)

The juice of half a lemon

2 or 3 cups of water (500 or 750 milliliters)

1 avocado

1 carrot

- In a non-stick frying pan, heat the olive oil on medium high heat. Add garlic, onion and cayenne pepper (chopped) and cook until golden brown.
- Add the tomatoes, tomato sauce, herbs and spices (cilantro, cumin, paprika and pepper), cooked quinoa, corn kernels, cooked red beans and 2 or 3 cups of water, making sure to cover all the ingredients. Cook for about 30 minutes over medium heat.
- When the chili is ready, add the lemon juice, stir and serve with avocado, carrot and vegan sour cream.

Per Serving: Calories: 353; Total Fat: 12g; Saturated Fat: 2g; Protein: 13g; Carbs: 50g; Fiber: 12g; Sugar: 8g

Super vegetable broth

Serves: 4 / Preparation time: 5 minutes / Cooking time: 1 Hour 30 minutes

1 or 2 tbsp extra virgin olive oil	2 leeks
4 cloves of garlic	1 potato
1 onion	2 bay leaves
2 turnips	8 cups water (2 liters)
2 carrots	1 or 2 tbsp soy sauce or tamari
1 celery stalk	

- Heat the oil in a pan over medium heat and when it's hot, add the veggies (chopped). Cook until golden brown.
- Add the bay leaves and the water and cook over high heat until the water starts to boil, then cook the broth over medium heat for 1 or 2 hours.
- Pour the broth through a strainer into a large heat-proof bowl or pot and discard solids. Add the soy sauce or tamari.

Per Serving: Calories: 13; Total Fat: 0.1g; Saturated Fat: 0g; Protein: 0.5g; Carbs: 2g; Fiber: 0g; Sugar: 1g

Chipotle Black Bean Tortilla Soup

Serves: 4 / Preparation time: 10 minutes / Cooking time: 35 minutes

SOUP

2 Tbsp avocado or coconut oil

1/2 white or yellow onion (diced)

3 cloves garlic (minced)

1/2 red or orange pepper (diced)

1 1/2 tsp cumin

1 tsp chili powder

1 1/2 cups Red Chipotle Salsa (or any blended or chunky spicy salsa)

4 cups vegetable stock (DIY or store-bought)

2 Tbsp coconut sugar or maple syrup (to taste) (optional)

2 15-ounce black beans (cooked in salt // slightly drained)

1 15.25-ounce whole kernel corn (drained)

FOR SERVING optional

Lime juice

Fresh cilantro (chopped)

Red onion (diced)

Tortilla chips

Ripe avocado (cubed)

Hot sauce

- Heat a large pot over medium heat. Once hot, add oil, garlic, onion, pepper, an a pinch each salt and pepper and stir. Cook for 4-5 minutes, stirring frequently, until onions are translucent and the peppers have a bit of color.
- Add cumin and chili powder and stir to coat. Then add salsa, vegetable stock and coconut sugar. Stir to combine, then increase heat to medium heat and bring to a low boil.
- Once it's boiling, add black beans and corn and stir. Reduce heat to low and simmer, covered, for 30 minutes or more, stirring occasionally. The longer it simmers, the more the flavor will develop. It's even better the next day.
- Serve as is or with recommended serving options above.
- Leftovers will keep covered in the refrigerator for 5-6 days or in the freezer for 1 month.

Per Serving: Calories: 265; Total Fat: 6g; Saturated Fat: 2g; Protein: 11g; Carbs: 51g; Fiber: 10g; Sugar: 11g

Vegan Broccoli Cheese Soup

Serves: 4 / Preparation time: 20 minutes / Cooking time: 20 minutes

Broccoli Cheese Soup

2 tablespoons vegan butter or coconut oil

1 large yellow onion, thinly sliced

3-4 cloves garlic

16 oz fresh or frozen broccoli, chopped and divided

1 large russet potato

3 cups vegetable broth

2 cups unsweetened soy milk

8 oz vegan cheddar cheese

3 tablespoons nutritional yeast

salt and pepper, to taste

OPTIONAL TOPPINGS

pan-fried onions

fresh broccoli florets

- In a large soup pan heat vegan butter and coconut oil over medium-high heat. Reduce heat to medium and add onions and garlic. Sauté for 5-7 minutes, stirring occasionally.
- Meanwhile, peel and chop potato and broccoli florets. Add potato and broccoli (reserving about 1 cup of broccoli) to soup and sauté another 3-4 minutes.
- Add broth and milk and bring to a low simmer. Simmer for 30 minutes, stirring occasionally, until broccoli and potatoes are tender.
- Stir in vegan cheese and nutritional yeast.
- Using an immersion blender (or food processor) blend soup until thick and creamy. Stir in reserved broccoli. Salt and pepper to taste.
- Serve immediately with fresh broccoli and pan-fried onions.

Per Serving: Calories: 271; Total Fat: 14g; Saturated Fat: 6g; Protein: 18g; Carbs: 27g; Fiber: 5g; Sugar: 3g

Grilled Tofu Miso Noodle Soup

Serves: 4 / Preparation time: 30 minutes / Cooking time: 20 minutes

Marinated Tofu
12 ounce block of extra-firm tofu
1 tablespoon water
1 tablespoon toasted sesame oil
1 tablespoon liquid aminos
1/2 teaspoon garlic powder
1/2 teaspoon onion powder
1/2 teaspoon agave nectar
1/4 teaspoon ground ginger
Pinch of salt post-grilling
Veggies
1 cup sliced red cabbage
1 cup sliced brussels sprouts
1 cup slivered red onion
2 cups broccoli florets bite-sized

Broth and Garnish
2 teaspoons toasted sesame oil
3 cloves garlic minced
2 teaspoons grated fresh ginger
4 cups vegetable broth
4 cups water
1/4 cup liquid aminos
6 ounces brown rice pad thai noodles
2 tablespoons white miso paste
1/4 cup cilantro chopped
1/4 cup diced green onion
2 teaspoons black sesame seeds
teaspoon Optional: 1 Hot Pepper Sesame
Oil for drizzling

- Marinated Tofu
- Drain tofu of water, wrap tightly in a clean cloth and press it, by putting heavy (STABLE) objects on top of it, for 15 to 20 minutes. While you are pressing the tofu, prep your vegetables.
- In a small bowl or ramekin, whisk together water, sesame oil, liquid aminos, garlic powder, onion powder, agave, and ginger until combined.
- Once most of the moisture is pressed out of your block of tofu, cut it into 32 pieces (or cut it into quarters, then those pieces in half for 8 rectangles, and lastly cutting those into quarters). Place pieces in a shallow container and pour marinade over the top, moving them around to get them coated. Marinate for 15 minutes, get started on grilling veggies and preparing broth.
- After the veggies are grilled, place tofu in panini press and grill until the marks are dark, pressing down gently ever couple of minutes. Once all tofu is grilled, turn off your press and leave it open with tofu on it to keep it warm until ready to assemble.
- Veggies, Broth and Assembly
- Heat a panini press until it reaches temp (mine has a green light and one temp, which I assume is fairly high). If you do not have one with non-stick coating, line with a thin coat of cooking oil spray. Place the slices of cabbage, brussels and red onion onto the press in a single layer; bring top down and grill until there are dark marks on each piece.
- While the veggies are cooking, warm toasted sesame oil in a large pot over medium heat. Once hot, add garlic and ginger to the pot and saute until the garlic begins to brown lightly. Add broth, water and liquid aminos to the pot and bring to a boil.
- Once boiling, add broccoli and rice noodles to the water, and cook according to the noodles packaging. Half way through, add in half of the grilled vegetables and continue to cook.
- When the noodles are tender, turn off stove and stir in miso paste until dissolved. Divide soup between four large soup/noodle bowls, then arrange remaining grilled vegetables, grilled tofu, cilantro, green onions, and black sesame seeds on top. Lastly, lightly drizzle Hot Pepper Sesame Oil over the top of each one and serve!

Per Serving: Calories: 271; Total Fat: 14g; Saturated Fat: 6g; Protein: 18g; Carbs: 27g; Fiber: 5g; Sugar: 3g

Vegan Minestrone

Serves: 4 / Preparation time: 10 minutes / Cooking time: 40 minutes

1 tsp olive oil

1/2 cup chopped onion chopped

4 cloves garlic chopped

1/2 cup chopped celery

3/4 cup chopped carrots

28 oz can diced tomato

15 oz can cannellini beans or other white beans or a combinationof white and kidney beans

1 cup chopped zucchini

3 cups water

1/2 tsp salt

1/2 tsp oregano

1/4 tsp thyme

1/4 tsp black pepper

1/2 cup elbows or other pasta use gluten-free if needed

1 cup baby spinach

3 tbsp chopped basil

vegan parmesan for garnish - optional

- Heat oil in a large saucepan over medium heat. Add onion and garlic and cook until translucent. 4 mins.
- Add celery, carrots and tomato and bring to a boil. 4 to 5 mins.
- Add the beans, zucchini, water, salt and spices and cook for 15 to 18 minutes.
- Add 1/2 cup pasta and simmer for 12 or more minutes. Taste and adjust salt, herbs and heat.
- Fold in spinach and 2 tbsp chopped basil and simmer for another minute. Serve hot garnished with fresh basil and vegan parmesan.

Per Serving: Calories: 210; Total Fat: 1g; Saturated Fat: 0g; Protein: 10g; Carbs: 42g; Fiber: 9g; Sugar: 7g

Easy Vegetarian Pho

Serves: 4 / Preparation time: 10 minutes / Cooking time: 40 minutes

2 star anise
1 cinnamon stick
1 tablespoon peppercorns
½ teaspoon whole cloves
5 cups water
½ small yellow onion, cut into 1" chunks
2 garlic cloves
1 2-inch piece of fresh ginger, sliced in half
4 ounces shiitake mushrooms, stems removed and reserved
3 tablespoons tamari

1 tablespoon rice vinegar
2 scallions, finely chopped
2 baby bok choy, sliced lengthwise into quarters
½ cup edamame (or protein of your choice)
4 ounces rice noodles
toppings:
lime slices
mung bean sprouts
fresh basil leaves
chile sauce (sambal or sriracha)

- In a medium pot over low heat, combine the star anise, cinnamon stick, peppercorns, and cloves and stir until fragrant, about 30 seconds.
- Add the water, onion, garlic, ginger, and the stems of the shiitake mushrooms. Simmer for 20 minutes, then strain and return the liquid back to the pot.
- Slice the shiitake mushroom caps and add them to the pot along with the tamari, rice vinegar, and scallions.
- Simmer 15 minutes, then add the bok choy and simmer until tender, about 8 minutes. Taste and adjust seasonings.
- In a pot of salted boiling water, prepare the noodles according to the package directions, cooking until al dente. Drain and rinse.
- Ladle pho into 2 bowls over the rice noodles. Serve with the lime slices, sprouts, basil, and chile sauce.

Per Serving: Calories: 353; Total Fat: 9g; Saturated Fat: 1g; Protein: 16g; Carbs: 54g; Fiber: 5g; Sugar: 10g

Roasted Cauliflower Soup

Serves: 4 / Preparation time: 10 minutes / Cooking time: 35 minutes

1 large head cauliflower, de-stemmed and florets broken up

1 1/2 tablespoon olive oil

salt & pepper to taste

5 cloves garlic, smashed with skins still on

1/2 large vidalia onion

2-3 sprigs thyme, stems removed

4 1/2 cups vegetable broth

- Preheat oven to 450 degrees F. Line a baking sheet with a silicone mat.
- Add the cauliflower to the baking sheet and 1 tablespoon olive oil, about ½ teaspoon salt and grind some pepper over it all. Using your hands, mixing it all in, massaging the ingredients into the cauliflower. Add the smashed garlic (skins still on) on the baking sheet. The skins help to prevent it burning; you'll remove thee afterwards. Roast for 15 minutes. I like to reserve a few pieces after roasting to top the soup with.
- Meanwhile, in a large high sided pot over medium high heat, sauté the onions in the ½ tablespoon olive oil until fragrant and browning, about 8 minutes, stirring infrequently.
- Add the roasted cauliflower, the garlic (skins remove), 2 sprigs of thyme and vegetable broth. Mix together with spatula.
- Bring to a boil, then reduce to a simmer for 15 minutes. Remove from heat and stir once more. If using an immersion blender, blend the soup together. If using a high powered blender, let cool slightly and add slowly to blender. Press the "soup" setting or blend on high until soup is thoroughly mixed and incorporated, at least 1 minute. Be careful that your soup is not too hot to crack your blender. Taste and salt and pepper to taste.
- Pour into bowls and top optionally with extra cauliflower, crushed red peppers, extra thyme and a drizzle of coconut milk. Enjoy!

Per Serving: Calories: 353; Total Fat: 9g; Saturated Fat: 1g; Protein: 16g; Carbs: 54g; Fiber: 5g; Sugar: 10g

Smoky Kale and Butter Bean Soup

Serves: 4 / Preparation time: 10 minutes / Cooking time: 35 minutes

1 tablespoon olive or coconut oil

2 cloves garlic, minced

1 medium yellow onion, chopped

2 cups red potatoes, cut into 1-inch cubes

4 cups vegetable broth

2 teaspoons smoked paprika

1 teaspoon salt

1/4 teaspoon black pepper

2 1/2 cups cooked butter (lima) beans

3 packed cups kale, stems removed

hemp seeds, for garnish

- Heat the oil in a large pot or dutch oven over medium heat. Sauté the garlic and onions together until fragrant, 3-5 minutes.
- Pour in the potatoes, vegetable broth, smoked paprika, salt and pepper. Continue cooking over low-medium heat about 20-30 minutes, until the potatoes are fork tender.
- Add in the beans, reserving a 1/2 cup to the side, and the kale. Stir to combine, and cook 5-10 more minutes. Remove from heat.
- Blend the soup with an immersion blender or in batches in a high-speed blender until smooth. Pour in the remaining butter beans and stir. Serve immediately with a garnish of hemp seeds or crackers!

Per Serving: Calories: 353; Total Fat: 9g; Saturated Fat: 1g; Protein: 16g; Carbs: 54g; Fiber: 5g; Sugar: 10g

Curried Beet Soup With Tandoori Chickpeas

Serves: 4 / Preparation time: 5 minutes / Cooking time: 25 minutes

CHICKPEAS
1 15-ounce can chickpeas (rinsed, drained + dried in a clean towel)
1 Tbsp melted coconut oil (or sub grape seed oil)
1/4 tsp sea salt (plus more to taste)
2 Tbsp tandoori masala spice blend
1 tsp coconut sugar
SOUP
1 Tbsp coconut or grape seed oil
2 medium shallots, thinly diced
2 cloves garlic, minced (2 cloves yield ~1 Tbsp)
1 Tbsp minced ginger
6 small-medium beets, peeled and quartered

1 pinch each sea salt + black pepper (plus more to taste)
1 1/2 Tbsp green curry paste (or sub 12 g curry powder per 25 g paste)
1/4 tsp ground cinnamon
1/2 tsp ground turmeric
1/2 tsp ground cumin
1/4 tsp cayenne pepper
1 pinch each ground cardamom and coriander (optional)
1 14-ounce can light coconut milk (optional // more for serving)
2 cups vegetable broth (store-bought)
2-3 Tbsp coconut sugar (or maple syrup)
Fresh chopped cilantro (optional)

- If preparing chickpeas, preheat oven to 375 degrees F (190 C), and add rinsed and dried chickpeas to a small mixing bowl. Top with coconut oil, salt, tandoori masala, and coconut sugar. Toss to combine, and sample a chickpea. Taste and adjust seasonings as needed.
- Spread onto a bare baking sheet and bake for 20-25 minutes, or until deep golden brown and fragrant. Set aside to cool.
- In the meantime, heat a large pot over medium heat.
- Once hot, add oil, shallots, garlic and ginger. Sauté for 2 minutes, stirring frequently.
- Add beets, salt and pepper, curry paste, cinnamon, turmeric, cumin, cayenne, cardamom and coriander (optional). Stir to coat, then cover and cook for 4 minutes, stirring occasionally.
- Add coconut milk, vegetable broth, and coconut sugar.
- Bring to a low boil over medium heat and then reduce heat to low, cover, and simmer for 15 minutes, or until beets are fork tender.
- Use an immersion blender, or transfer soup to a blender, and purée on high until creamy and smooth. If using a blender, return soup back to pot.
- Taste and adjust seasonings as needed, adding more dry spices, salt, or sweetener to taste. I didn't make any adjustments.
- Serve with an extra drizzle of coconut milk (optional), a generous amount of tandoori chickpea, and a sprinkle of cilantro (optional).
- Store leftover soup covered in the refrigerator for 3-4 days or in the freezer up to 1 month. Store chickpeas separately in a well-sealed container at room temperature up to 2 days.

Per Serving: Calories: 327; Total Fat: 15g; Saturated Fat: 10g; Protein: 10g; Carbs: 42g; Fiber: 7g; Sugar: 20g

Golden Lentil Barley Soup

Serves: 4 / Preparation time: 10 minutes / Cooking time: 25 minutes

1/2 tbsp extra-virgin olive oil or refined coconut oil
1 medium yellow or white onion finely chopped
4 cloves garlic minced
1 inch ginger root minced or grated
1 inch fresh turmeric root minced or grated (or use 1/2 teaspoon ground turmeric)
2 carrots peeled and diced or thinly sliced
1/4 tsp ground cumin heaping
1/4 tsp ground coriander heaping

4 and 1/2 cups low-sodium vegetable broth
3/4 cups dry red lentils rinsed
1/2 cup dry pearl barley rinsed several times in hot water
2 tbsp tomato paste
1/2 tsp salt scant (plus more to taste)
ground black pepper to taste (I used just a pinch)
3 cups loosely-packed fresh baby spinach leaves (or more, if you like - up to 6 ounces)
(optional) fresh lemon juice, for serving

- Warm the oil in a large pot. Add the onion and a pinch of salt, and saute until translucent, stirring occasionally; 3-5 minutes.
- Add the garlic, ginger, and fresh turmeric (if using), stir, and cook for another about 60 seconds or until softened and fragrant.
- Stir in the carrot, ground turmeric (if using), ground cumin, and ground coriander. Cook for 2-3 minutes more, stirring occasionally, until the spices are fragrant and the carrot softened slightly.
- Add the vegetable broth, red lentils, and pearl barley to the pot. Bring to a boil, then reduce to a simmer. Cook uncovered for about 20 minutes, or until the lentils and barley are both cooked through.
- Stir in the tomato paste, and season to taste with salt and pepper.
- Stir in the spinach, turn off the heat and cover the pot with a lid. Remove after 2-3 minutes, or when the spinach is wilted to your preference.
- Serve hot, with a light squeeze of fresh lemon juice if desired.

Per Serving: Calories: 315; Total Fat: 2g; Saturated Fat: 1g; Protein: 16g; Carbs: 60g; Fiber: 15g; Sugar: 5g

Roasted Garlic Tomato Soup

Serves: 4 / Preparation time: 10 minutes / Cooking time: 25 minutes

For the roasted garlic:
1 medium head garlic
Olive oil, for drizzling
Salt and pepper, for sprinkling
For the soup:
1 tablespoon olive oil
1 medium sweet onion, chopped
1 tablespoon tomato paste
1 pint cherry tomatoes

1 (14 ounce) can fire-roasted diced tomatoes
1 1/2 cups low-sodium vegetable broth
1/2 cup canned full-fat coconut milk
1/4 teaspoon salt
1/4 teaspoon pepper
1/2 teaspoon dried oregano
Chopped fresh basil, for serving
Crusty bread, for serving

- For the roasted garlic:
- Preheat the oven to 375ºF.
- Cut the top end off the head of garlic, so that the bulb remains intact and the cloves are exposed. Remove any of the papery loose outer layers. Place the garlic on a piece of aluminum foil, then drizzle with olive oil and sprinkle with salt and pepper. Wrap it in the foil then bake for about 50 to 55 minutes, until tender and the cloves are golden brown. Remove it from the oven, and once it is cool enough to handle, squeeze the cloves out of the peel, then use a fork to mash them into a paste. Measure out 1 tablespoon of the mashed garlic to use in the soup. Any extra can be stored in an airtight container in the fridge.
- For the soup:
- Add the olive oil to a large stockpot or Dutch oven set over medium heat. When hot, add in the onion and cook for about 5 to 6 minutes, until tender. Stir in the tomato paste. Add the cherry tomatoes, diced tomatoes (with their juices), broth, coconut milk, salt, pepper, oregano and the 1 tablespoon roasted garlic to the pot. Mix to combine then bring to a simmer. Reduce the heat and continue simmering for about 15 to 20 minutes, to allow the flavors to meld and the cherry tomatoes to soften and break down. Remove from the heat.
- Carefully transfer the soup to a blender and process until smooth. Return the soup to the pot. Taste and season with additional salt and pepper as needed. Serve garnished with fresh basil and bread on the side for dipping.

Per Serving: Calories: 160; Total Fat: 11g; Saturated Fat: 6g; Protein: 3g; Carbs: 12g; Fiber: 1g; Sugar: 3g

Carrot Soup With Carrot Top Pesto

Serves: 4 / Preparation time: 10 minutes / Cooking time: 50 minutes

1 tablespoon extra-virgin olive oil

1 cup chopped yellow onions

3 garlic cloves, smashed

2 heaping cups chopped carrots

1½ teaspoons grated fresh ginger

1 tablespoon apple cider vinegar or freshly squeezed orange juice

3 to 4 cups vegetable broth

1 teaspoon maple syrup, or to taste (optional)

coconut milk for garnish (optional)

- Heat the olive oil in a large pot over medium heat. Add the onions and a generous pinch of salt and pepper and cook until softened, stirring occasionally, about 8 minutes. Add the smashed garlic cloves (they'll get blended later) and chopped carrots to the pot and cook about 8 minutes more, stirring occasionally.
- Stir in the ginger, then add the apple cider vinegar, and then add 3 to 4 cups of broth, depending on your desired consistency. Reduce to a simmer and cook until the carrots are soft, about 30 minutes.
- Let cool slightly and transfer to a blender. Blend until smooth. Taste and adjust seasonings. Add maple syrup, if desired.
- Serve the soup with the pesto on the side. Garnish with a drizzle of coconut milk, if desired.

Per Serving: Calories: 160; Total Fat: 11g; Saturated Fat: 6g; Protein: 3g; Carbs: 12g; Fiber: 1g; Sugar: 3g

Roasted Asparagus Basil Soup

Serves: 4 / Preparation time: 15 minutes / Cooking time: 25 minutes

14- 16 Asparagus Spears

2 cloves of garlic

1/2 white or red onion thick slices

oil, salt and pepper as needed

1/2 cup soaked cashews or 1/2 cup cashew cream

2 cups water or vegetable broth

1/2 tsp dried dill or 2 tsp fresh dill

1/4 cup packed basil leaves

2 tsp extra virgin olive oil

1/4 tsp salt or taste

2 tsp nutritional yeast

a very generous dash of black pepper

- Preheat the oven to 450 degrees F / 220ºc.
- Remove the hard stems from the Asparagus spread. Chop the Asparagus spears into 2 inch pieces. Place on parchment lined sheet. Place garlic cloves and onion in the center of the sheet. Spray or brush oil. Sprinkle salt and pepper and bake for 12 to 15 minutes. Remove the garlic at 10 minutes if already golden.
- Cool slightly, then blend with the cashews, broth, dill, basil, olive oil, salt and nutritional yeast.
- Add blended puree to a pan and heat at medium-high heat and bring to a boil. Stir frequently. 8 - 10 minutes.
- Taste and adjust salt. Add more water/broth if needed for desired consistency.
- Garnish with cashew cream and black pepper. I blended the cashews with some basil, lemon juice, salt, pepper for a herbed cashew cream drizzle. or add some sour cream and onion clusters.

Per Serving: Calories: 290; Total Fat: 16g; Saturated Fat: 3g; Protein: 12g; Carbs: 23g; Fiber: 7g; Sugar: 7g

Roasted Garlic and Red Pepper Soup

Serves: 4 / Preparation time: 15 minutes / Cooking time: 25 minutes

3 large bell peppers

1 head of garlic

2 cups of vegetable stock or water

2 tbsp of soaked pine nuts

1 tsp dried basil or a few fresh ones

salt, pepper

- Put the whole garlic head and the peppers on a baking tray and bake them for about 30 minutes at 200°C. Once they are ready let them cool a bit, so you don't burn yourself.
- Peel and deseed the peppers, squeeze the garlic cloves out of their skins and add everything to a blender. Blend until smooth. Add more water if it would be too thick.
- Pour the mixture into a sauce pan, heat it up a bit and serve warm. Enjoy!

Per Serving: Calories: 220; Total Fat: 16g; Saturated Fat: 9g; Protein: 4g; Carbs: 16g; Fiber: 4g; Sugar: 9g

Oyster Mushroom Wonton Soup With Wilted Kale

Serves: 4 / Preparation time: 15 minutes / Cooking time: 0 minutes

For the wontons

4 cups oyster mushroom caps, minced

1 TB Earth Balance

25-40 wonton wrappers

For the broth

2 cups homemade stock or Imagine brand No-Chicken broth

1 TB toasted sesame oil

1 TB soy sauce or tamari

To serve

handful of chopped kale

1 scallion, chopped

sriracha, to taste

- First, cut away the tough stems from the oyster mushrooms, then mince the soft caps, then rinse and drain well under cold water.
- Reserve and freeze the inedible but flavorful stems for making stock later, if you wish.
- To make your wonton filling, melt the Earth Balance in a large, flat-bottomed skillet over medium heat. Throw in the minced oyster mushrooms and saute until almost all of the liquid has reduced from the pan. Remove from the heat and set aside to cool. Then, assemble your wontons following these steps.
- Place the wontons onto a baking sheet lined with a silpat so they are not touching each other, and put into the freezer for at least a hour. Transfer to a container or Ziploc bag to store.
- When you are ready to make your soup, remove a few wontons from the freezer. (No need to defrost them.) Heat the broth in a small saucepan, then add in the sesame oil and soy sauce. Throw in the wontons and allow to heat through until softened and translucent, about 5 minutes, taking care to ensure they don't stick to the bottom of the saucepan.
- Add in the kale and any other chopped vegetables as desired, and drizzle with sriracha. Serve immediately with hot tea.

Per Serving: Calories: 231; Total Fat: 9g; Saturated Fat: 3g; Protein: 17g; Carbs: 19g; Fiber: 1g; Sugar: 2g

DESSERTS

Contents

Vegan Blueberry Peach Crisp

Serves: 4 / Preparation time: 15 minutes / Cooking time: 55 minutes

FOR THE CRISP

2 cups frozen peaches

4 cups frozen blueberries

1/4 cup sugar

2 tablespoons corn starch

1/4 teaspoon salt

1/2 teaspoon cinnamon

FOR THE TOPPING

3/4 cup brown sugar

1/2 cup gluten free oat flour

3/4 cup gluten free rolled oats

1/4 teaspoon salt

2 tablespoons coconut oil, melted

1/4 cup vegan butter, melted

- In a large bowl, mix together all ingredients for the crisp. You may need to let the berries thaw for 5-10 minutes and stir until the remaining ingredients stick to the fruit
- In a separate bowl, make the crisp topping
- Mix together all ingredients until it resembles wet sand
- Pour crisp ingredients into a pie dish
- Sprinkle topping evenly over the top
- Bake at 350 degrees for 50-60 minutes, or until bubbling and the top starts to brown
- Allow to rest for 10-15 minutes
- Serve with ice cream

Per Serving: Calories: 288; Total Fat: 11g; Saturated Fat: 7g; Protein: 3g; Carbs: 48g; Fiber: 4g; Sugar: 33g

No Bake Peanut Butter Truffles

Serves: 4 / Preparation time: 20 minutes / Cooking time: 0 minutes

FOR THE TRUFFLE FILLING:

3/4 cup all natural creamy peanut butter

1/4 cup pure grade A maple syrup

1 tablespoon coconut palm sugar

1/4 cup coconut flour (see instructions before adding)

1/8 teaspoon sea salt

FOR THE CHOCOLATE SHELL:

1 cup semi sweet chocolate chips

1/2 teaspoon coconut oil

1/4 teaspoon sea salt

- Use a mixer to beat together peanut butter, maple syrup, coconut palm sugar, and salt for the filling.
- Add in coconut flour slowly, until the mixture is not wet but not very dry. It should be easy to roll the balls without the mixture sticking to your hands. This will depend on your peanut butter texture how much flour to add. I used 1/4 cup of coconut flour as my peanut butter was drippy.
- Roll filling into small balls and place on a cookie sheet
- Freeze for 5 minutes to chill slightly
- Melt coconut oil and chocolate in the microwave (be careful not to burn)
- Once melted, stir in the salt
- Drop peanut butter balls into the chocolate, and use a spoon to drip the chocolate over the balls.
- Use a fork to get the balls back out and onto the cookie sheet. (look up a tutorial for necessary, but it's really quite easy!)
- Freeze truffles until chocolate is set.
- Store in the freezer for best results

Per Serving: Calories: 161; Total Fat: 11g; Saturated Fat: 4g; Protein: 3g; Carbs: 15g; Fiber: 2g; Sugar: 11g

Vegan Peanut Butter Cups

Serves: 4 / Preparation time: 20 minutes / Cooking time: 0 minutes

FOR THE CHOCOLATE LAYER

10 oz bag of semi sweet dairy free chocolate chips

2 tablespoons virgin coconut oil

1/4 teaspoon sea salt

1/4 teaspoon vanilla extract

FOR THE PEANUT BUTTER FILLING

3/4 cup all natural peanut butter, chilled in the fridge (only ingredients should be peanuts and salt)

1/4 cup pure maple syrup

1/4 teaspoon sea salt

1 tablespoon coconut palm sugar

- Add 2 tablespoons of coconut oil to a saucepan and heat on low heat, until melted
- Add 10 oz bag of chocolate chips, stirring on low heat, until melted (can take 5 minutes) *be sure not to burn chocolate and only melt on low*
- Once chocolate is melted, add in 1/4 teaspoon sea salt and 1/4 teaspoon vanilla extract
- Once chocolate mixture is stirred and melted, line a 12 cup muffin tin with paper muffin liners
- Pour 1 tablespoon of chocolate mixture in the bottom of each muffin liner
- Place muffin tin in freezer for 10-15 minutes, or until chocolate is set
- While chocolate is hardening, make the peanut butter mixture
- Add 3/4 cup of chilled peanutbutter (see note above) to a bowl *note - peanut butter should be thick not drippy)
- Add maple syrup, sea salt, and coconut palm sugar and stir with a fork until well combined
- Remove muffin tin from freezer and place 1 tablespoon of peanut butter mixture on top of each layer of chocolate
- Drizzle one teaspoon of chocolate mixture over the tops of each muffin cup, making sure to cover the tops well
- Freeze for 15 minutes, or until chocolate is set
- Store in freezer or fridge (note - if left in freezer long leave out for a minute or so to soften slightly)

Per Serving: Calories: 251; Total Fat: 17g; Saturated Fat: 8g; Protein: 5g; Carbs: 16g; Fiber: 2g; Sugar: 19g

Chocolate Sea Salt Pretzel Bark

Serves: 4 / Preparation time: 5 minutes / Cooking time: 0 minutes

10 oz dairy free dark chocolate chunks or chips

1 tablespoon + 1 teaspoon coconut oil

1 teaspoon Nielsen-Massey Madagascar Bourbon Pure Vanilla Extract

1 teaspoon flaked sea salt

1/2 cup roughly chopped gluten free pretzels

15 - 20 gluten free pretzels, for topping

- In a medium sized sauce pan, heat coconut oil and chocolate chunks over low heat until melted, stirring often (around 3 - 5 minutes)
- Remove from heat and stir in chopped pretzels and vanilla extract
- Line an 8 X 8 baking dish with wax paper and pour the chocolate mixture in
- Use a rubber spatula to spread it evenly into all the corners of the pan
- Sprinkle on sea salt and top with whole pretzels, as pictured
- Freeze for 1 hour, or until set
- Chop into small pieces using a knife, or break with your hands
- Store in an airtight container in the fridge or freezer

Per Serving: Calories: 258; Total Fat: 8g; Saturated Fat: 4g; Protein: 5g; Carbs: 53g; Fiber: 2g; Sugar: 9g

Chocolate Chip Cookies

Serves: 4 / Preparation time: 10 minutes / Cooking time: 12 minutes

2 1/4 cups whole wheat pastry flour	1/3 cup unsweetened applesauce
1 teaspoon salt	1 teaspoon baking powder
1 teaspoon baking soda	1/2 cup vegan butter, softened
1/2 cup pure cane sugar	1/2 cup coconut oil, melted
2/3 cup brown sugar	10 0z dairy free dark chocolate chips

- Whisk flour, salt, baking soda, and baking powder until combined. Set aside
- In a large bowl, cream together sugar, brown sugar, applesauce, vegan butter, and coconut oil
- Add the dry ingredients to the wet, and beat to combine
- Fold in chocolate chips
- Drop by rounded spoonfuls onto a baking sheet
- Bake at 350 degrees for 10 - 14 minutes, until browned

Per Serving: Calories: 203; Total Fat: 10g; Saturated Fat: 7g; Protein: 4g; Carbs: 27g; Fiber: 2g; Sugar: 10g

DIY Vegan Magic Shell

Serves: 4 / Preparation time: 1 minutes / Cooking time: 2 minutes

3/4 cup dairy free chocolate chips or chunks

1 tablespoon all natural creamy peanut butter

2 teaspoons coconut oil

- Add all ingredients to a bowl and microwave until completely melted, checking and stirring every 20-30 seconds.
- Serve poured over ice cream or frozen dessert of choice

Per Serving: Calories: 268; Total Fat: 19g; Saturated Fat: 11g; Protein: 3g; Carbs: 30g; Fiber: 3g; Sugar: 24g

Strawberry Banana Smoothie

Serves: 4 / Preparation time: 1 minutes / Cooking time: 2 minutes

4 cups frozen strawberries

1 cup frozen banana chunks

1 cup milk of choice (vegan)

- Add the milk to the bottom of your high speed blender
- Add strawberries and frozen bananas on top of the milk
- Blend, scraping down the edges if necessary

Per Serving: Calories: 184; Total Fat: 2g; Saturated Fat: 1g; Protein: 5g; Carbs: 47g; Fiber: 2g; Sugar: 19g

Almond Butter Cups

Serves: 4 / Preparation time: 10 minutes / Cooking time: 5 minutes

10 oz semi sweet dairy free chocolate chips

2 tablespoons coconut oil

1/2 teaspoon vanilla extract

2/3 cup creamy almond butter

2 tablespoons maple syrup

5 teaspoons coconut flour

1/4 teaspoon sea salt

Flaked sea salt, for topping

- Add chocolate chips and coconut oil to a medium sized sauce pan
- Turn heat on low or medium, and heat until melted, stirring frequently to avoid burning
- Once melted, stir in the vanilla extract
- Line a muffin tin with 12 parchment paper muffin cups
- Add 2 teaspoons of the chocolate mixture to the bottom of each muffin cup
- Once finished, shake the pan down to make sure chocolate lays flat in each cup
- Place muffin tin in freezer for 10 - 15 minutes, until chocolate hardens
- While chocolate is hardening, combine the almond butter, maple syrup, coconut flour, and 1/4 teaspoon of sea salt. Use a fork or your hands to combine (the mixture should be dry enough to not stick to your hands)
- Once chocolate hardens, distribute almond butter mixture evenly into each of the 12 tins, and use your hands to flatten it down
- Pour remaining chocolate over the tops, around 1 1/2 - 2 teaspoons per cup, until all of your chocolate is used up
- Sprinkle tops generously with flaked sea salt
- Place tin back in freezer for around 15 minutes, or until chocolate is hardened
- Store the almond butter cups in the fridge or freezer

Per Serving: Calories: 284; Total Fat: 18g; Saturated Fat: 4g; Protein: 4g; Carbs: 20g; Fiber: 3g; Sugar: 19g

Double Chocolate Milkshake

Serves: 4 / Preparation time: 5 minutes / Cooking time: 0 minutes

1 large sweet potato, peeled and diced (about 2 cups) - steamed and frozen

2 tablespoons cacao powder

2 tablespoons mini chocolate chips

3 tablespoons pure maple syrup

1 1/4 cups unsweetened vanilla almond milk

- For the sweet potatoes, I prepped the day before. Simple peel and dice one large sweet potato and steam until fork tender
- Once cooled, transfer to a ziploc bag and freeze (overnight preferably)
- Add all ingredients to a blender and blend on high until well combined
- garnish with additional chocolate chips, if desired

Per Serving: Calories: 234; Total Fat: 6g; Saturated Fat: 2g; Protein: 4g; Carbs: 45g; Fiber: 4g; Sugar: 28g

Peanut Butter Fudge

Serves: 4 / Preparation time: 5 minutes / Cooking time: 5 minutes

1 1/2 cups creamy peanut butter (only ingredients: peanuts + salt)

6 tablespoons coconut oil, measured while solid

1/2 cup pure maple syrup

2 teaspoons vanilla extract

2 tablespoons coconut flour

1/2 teaspoon sea salt

- Combine peanut butter, coconut oil, maple syrup, vanilla extract, and salt in a medium sized sauce pan
- Whisk on low heat until thoroughly combined (2-3 minutes)
- Whisk in coconut flour
- Line an 8 by 8 dish with wax paper
- Pour fudge into the lined dish and spread evenly with a rubber spatula
- Allow to set 1 hour in the freezer
- Lift wax paper up to remove the fudge, then cut into pieces
- Return to freezer to store
- Serve chilled for best texture

Per Serving: Calories: 117; Total Fat: 14g; Saturated Fat: 6g; Protein: 4g; Carbs: 10g; Fiber: 1g; Sugar: 6g

4 Ingredient Chocolate Banana Ice Cream

Serves: 4 / Preparation time: 5 minutes / Cooking time: 0 minutes

3 cups frozen banana chunks

2 tablespoons all natural peanut butter

1/4 cup raw cacao powder

2 tablespoons pure maple syrup

- Add all ingredients to a high speed blender or food processor and blend until totally smooth, scraping down as necessary.
- Add a splash of milk if needed, but the less liquid used the thicker your ice cream will be

Per Serving: Calories: 490; Total Fat: 11g; Saturated Fat: 2g; Protein: 10g; Carbs: 90g; Fiber: 12g; Sugar: 46g

Strawberry Pineapple Freezer Pops

Serves: 4 / Preparation time: 10 minutes / Cooking time: 0 minutes

10 oz frozen strawberries

10 oz frozen pineapple

3 cups coconut water

4 tablespoons pure maple syrup

- Add All ingredients to a high speed blender and blend until smooth
- Pour into popsicle bags (recipe will yield 15 popsicles)
- Seal bags and place flat in the freezer
- Freeze until solid

Per Serving: Calories: 46; Total Fat: 0g; Saturated Fat: 0g; Protein: 1g; Carbs: 11g; Fiber: 1g; Sugar: 9g

Easy Peach Crisp

Serves: 4 / Preparation time: 5 minutes / Cooking time: 55 minutes

FOR THE CRISP

30 oz frozen peaches, thawed slightly

1/4 cup brown sugar

1/4 cup coconut sugar

3 tablespoons corn starch

1/2 teaspoon salt

3/4 teaspoon cinnamon

1/4 teaspoon nutmeg

FOR THE CRISP TOPPING

1 1/4 cups brown sugar

1 cup whole wheat pastry flour

1 1/4 cups rolled oats

1/2 teaspoon salt

3 tablespoons coconut oil, melted

1/2 cup vegan butter, melted

- In a large bowl, combine all ingredients for the crisp
- You will need to stir until the ingredients stick to the peaches (usually after around 10 minutes of allowing the peaches to thaw)
- In a separate bowl, combine ingredients for the crisp topping and stir until it resembles wet sand
- Pour crisp ingredients into a baking dish and spoon the crisp topping in an even layer over the top
- Bake at 350 degrees for 50-60 minutes, or until bubbly and browned
- Serve with vanilla ice cream

Per Serving: Calories: 460; Total Fat: 16g; Saturated Fat: 10g; Protein: 7g; Carbs: 70g; Fiber: 5g; Sugar: 40g

THE "DIRTY DOZEN" AND "CLEAN 15"

Every year, the Environmental Working Group releases a list of the produce with the most pesticide residue (Dirty Dozen) and a list of the ones with the least **chance of having residue (Clean 15). It's based on analysis from the U.S.** Department of Agriculture Pesticide Data Program report.

The Environmental Working Group found that 70% of the 48 types of produce tested had residues of at least one type of pesticide. In total there were 178 different pesticides and pesticide breakdown products. This residue can stay on veggies and fruit even after they are washed and peeled. All pesticides are toxic to humans and consuming them can cause damage to the nervous system, reproductive system, cancer, a weakened immune system, and more. Women who are pregnant can expose their unborn children to toxins through their diet, and continued exposure to pesticides can affect their development.

This info can help you choose the best fruits and veggies, as well as which ones you should always try to buy organic.

The Dirty Dozen

- Strawberries
- Spinach
- Nectarines
- Apples
- Peaches
- Celery
- Grapes
- Pears
- Cherries
- Tomatoes
- Sweet bell peppers
- Potatoes

The Clean 15

- Sweet corn
- Avocados
- Pineapples
- Cabbage
- Onions
- Frozen sweet peas
- Papayas
- Asparagus
- Mangoes
- Eggplant
- Honeydew
- Kiwi
- Cantaloupe
- Cauliflower
- Grapefruit

MEASUREMENT CONVERSION TABLES

VOLUME EQUIVALENTS (DRY)

US Standard	Metric (Approx.)
¼ teaspoon	1 ml
½ teaspoon	2 ml
1 teaspoon	5 ml
1 tablespoon	15 ml
¼ cup	59 ml
½ cup	118 ml
1 cup	235 ml

WEIGHT EQUIVALENTS

US Standard	Metric (Approx.)
½ ounce	15 g
1 ounce	30 g
2 ounces	60 g
4 ounces	115 g
8 ounces	225 g
12 ounces	340 g
16 oz or 1 lb	455 g

VOLUME EQUIVALENTS (LIQUID)

US Standard	US Standard (ounces)	Metric (Approx.)
2 tablespoons	1 fl oz	30 ml
¼ cup	2 fl oz	60 ml
½ cup	4 fl oz	120 ml
1 cup	8 fl oz	240 ml
1 ½ cups	12 fl oz	355 ml
2 cups or 1 pint	16 fl oz	475 ml
4 cups or 1 quart	32 fl oz	1 L
1 gallon	128 fl oz	4 L

OVEN TEMPERATURES

Fahrenheit (F)	Celsius (C) (Approx)
250°F	120°C
300°F	150°C
325°F	165°C
350°F	180°C
375°F	190°C
400°F	200°C
425°F	220°C
450°F	230°C

Made in United States
North Haven, CT
06 December 2021